BUILDING BETTER RELATIONSHIPS

A Guidebook for Men

JAMES SWANIGER

ISBN: 1-4392-2226-6
ISBN-13: 9781439222263

LCCN: 2009900455

Visit www.booksurge.com to order additional copies.

Contents

To Tim and Judy
Thank you for your care, guidance, and teaching.

Foreword

"*Building Better Relationships* focuses on what most men want, yet many struggle to attain—personal fulfillment—at home, work, in the community, and with themselves. Jim Swaniger has written a practical guide that is well suited for those men who look outside themselves for fulfillment, and teaches them how to access and apply their existing internal resources. Its "on-the-job-training" approach is non-threatening and familiar to many men. This mindset helps offset reader resistance, awkwardness, or embarrassment related to emotional learning. Its self-study design helps mental health professionals assign homework to accommodate clients who have irregular schedules."

Lawrence E. Hedges, Ph.D., Founding Director, Newport Psychoanalytic Institute, Tustin, CA., Director of the Listening Perspectives Study Center, Orange, CA., Assistant Professor, University of California, Irvine, Medical School, Department of Psychiatry, and author of *Facing the Challenge of Liability in Psychotherapy; Interpreting the Countertransference; In Search of the Lost Mother of Infancy; Listening Perspectives in Psychotherapy; Remembering, Repeating, and Working Through Childhood Trauma; Strategic Emotional Involvement; Terrifying Transferences,* and *Working the Organizing Experience.*

Preface

I began this book with the goal of helping men self-improve. I thought recovering from decades of substance abuse, being a former engineer and now a licensed psychotherapist separated me from other men. But along the way this changed. I realized I'm still a work-in-progress with just one difference—I have peace of mind. And if you read this book and do what's asked, the same can happen for you.

Early on I thought this book would change *who* men are, but in time realized this was a bad idea. Neither I nor anyone else should be so arrogant. What I do have is the wisdom gained from thirty years of recovery, self-exploration, and self-improvement, and this qualifies me to help men change *how* they are. Some call this wisdom "street credibility." Whatever it's called, I'm at a place and time in life when giving back is important. And what I have to give you is the opportunity for a better life and better relationships; to teach you all I know about your innate capacity for personal fulfillment.

Before working at self-improvement, I was like most guys I knew: easily annoyed when asked to talk about feelings or committed relationships. To me, this felt like an interrogation. If I couldn't change the subject, I'd get aggravated and walk away. If I had to stay, I'd get angry. Sometimes this escalated and I'd drink. Sometimes I'd rage and scare people. I didn't care; I only knew I hated feeling foolish, ashamed, embarrassed, or cornered by things I knew nothing about. Eventually, life pushed back—friends, family, coworkers began leaving. One night my life drastically changed—I woke up in jail with another drunk rummaging through my pants pockets.

Luckily, a part of me was still sane enough to get help. Therapy, community support groups, and a desire to not die from alcohol poisoning supplied my motivation. I found, as you will, that emotions and feelings aren't that hard to understand or talk about or to make part of your daily life. It's like learning to ride a bicycle or to swim; once you learn, it becomes second nature. But in the beginning, you have to work hard.

Self-improvement is like any other job, and this book breaks it down into manageable pieces. I recommend reading one page at a time, doing one exercise at a time, putting one foot in front of the other, one day at a time, and I guarantee you'll feel different about yourself when you've finished.

As a relational therapist, I help others build connections. While writing, I found myself doing the same—I imagined a small group of men talking about self-improvement, being better partners at home, better coworkers at the office, and more helpful in the community. So as you read along, I invite you to imagine being part of such a group. The clients you'll read about are composites of many men I've worked with, and any similarity to any person is accidental.

Finally, when a client of mine searches for hope or understanding sometimes I'll talk about my journey. Here, I do the same; when you're asked to do an exercise or learn a skill that I found helpful, I'll let you know. For instance, I'll point out the exercises that helped me stop drinking and raging.

Acknowledgments

I have been honored and privileged to work with hundreds of clients in their journeys toward personal fulfillment and better relationships. This book emerged from this experience. To the men who took me onto their emotional battlefields, as well as the women who helped me understand men through their eyes and hearts, I extend my warmest gratitude.

New authors need guidance from dedicated professionals, and I have learned a great deal from my writing coach Bruce McAllister and my brilliant editor Brady Kahn. I also want to thank Jen Baranick for her encouragement and editorial contributions during this book's development.

I am grateful to Susan Clarke, LMFT, Mark Goodman, M.D., Larry Hedges, Ph.D., and Mark MacMillin, Psy.D., for their critiques and insightful suggestions during this project.

Finally, my unending gratitude to Dan Gumbleton, LCSW, for giving me the hope I needed to overcome my addictions thirty years ago.

Introduction

Have you ever wondered…?

- Why do my relationships always end the same way?
- Why it is that my life never gets any better?
- Why can't I commit to a relationship?

Has your partner complained about any of the following?

- You are not emotionally available!
- You do not hear me!
- You are not the man I married!
- If you loved me, you would know what I want!

Were you angered or frustrated by these complaints?

Most men have been there. They wonder why they keep hearing the same complaints and why life never improves. In my own case, before I changed careers from engineering to psychology, questions or complaints like these left me feeling confused and frustrated.

What got you to this point is your own story. Perhaps your partner has threatened to leave unless you become more emotionally available or unless you start to hear what she or he says. Perhaps others have said you need to deal with your rage, or it has begun to even scare you. Perhaps your work performance is getting worse or your coworkers complain about your lack of cooperation. Perhaps you have had a series of unsuccessful dating relationships. Perhaps you are sober and want to know what drives you to drink. Perhaps you have gambled away your savings. Perhaps you're finally recognizing you play a part in what goes wrong in your life. Perhaps you are simply fed up with feeling the way you do.

This book will help you understand why you feel stuck in life, and why you react a certain way at particular times. One way of doing this is to direct you in exercises known as "guided imagery" that will help you develop and use your imagination, so you can begin seeing your way to a better life. You'll also gain insight into how you approach life and relationships, such as when you're using outdated and ineffective patterns without knowing it. You'll learn how to identify when you're doing this and why it feels natural to you. You'll learn why this happens most often in your closest relationships. And you'll learn how to stop.

You'll begin self-improvement using an approach similar to on-the-job-training. I've nicknamed this effort *bridge-building* because you'll be reconnecting with parts of your inner self you may not be aware of; parts that have always been available to help you.

This work may be a bit difficult at times, especially if this is your first experience with self-improvement. But the payoff is worthwhile—a life of more contentment, peace, fun, and better relationships.

As little boys, we may have felt some fear while learning to swim or to ride a bicycle, but we felt the fear and did it anyway; what we wanted to learn demanded this. Even later on in life, it's natural to feel nervous when learning something new, but nervousness soon gives way to confidence, and new habits become second nature. Because working on self-improvement and "relating" may be new to you, you may feel awkward with these topics. You might feel some anxiety when you start. If you need help with this, you'll learn ways to manage apprehension early on in this book.

Feeling a strong reaction, like anger or anxiety, rarely happens when you read a self-improvement book. Still, as you read this book, if you have uncomfortable thoughts, feelings, or other reactions, pause, put the book aside and let the reaction pass. Then, start reading again. If the same topic continues to distress you, skip over it and return to it later, or you can avoid reading the topic altogether. You can also go on-line to learn how to get immediate help for anxiety at these websites:

http://www.apa.org/topics/topicanxiety.html

http://www.anxiety.com

http://www.adaa.org

You'll learn more about coping with anxiety in chapter 2.

You'll have opportunities to enjoy this work too. Using guided imagery, sometimes you will intentionally imagine different scenes from your past; at other times, pictures will automatically appear in your mind; at yet other times, you'll feel as though you're dreaming. All of this can be enjoyable.

In the same way that remembering a dream can help you to understand your life, the use of guided imagery and your reactions to it are valuable to your self-discovery. And, self-discovery plays a major part in feeling fulfilled. Like your first successful bike ride or your first swim, self-improvement work can be energizing; you'll spend time in a place inside yourself where your capacity for fulfillment lives and is ready to go to work. And I assure you, once you're in this place, it can feel like you've found an oil well in your backyard!

It's a good idea to record your experiences when doing self-improvement work. If you're like me, remembering important ideas or thoughts for a few days or a week doesn't always happen. So you're encouraged to keep progress notes at several key points; this is a proven way to give your efforts traction. Keeping a record helps you track

- changes in your self-confidence
- changes in others' reactions to you
- new ideas about yourself and your relationships
- what works and what doesn't

Along the way, you'll read true stories of men who've been in your place and went where you're headed. When you've finished this book, you'll understand why parts of your life don't work, why they sometimes hurt, what you can do to change this, how to do this, and when.

You'll notice that male and female genders are intermixed throughout this book. This is done with the deepest respect for all relationship choices.

Sit back and get comfortable. Just like meeting with long-lost friends, you're about to reconnect with parts of yourself you probably didn't know existed. Make sure you have pencil and paper nearby. If you prefer, there are blank pages at the back of this book for progress notes.

Chapter 1
Bridge Building

The capacity for personal fulfillment lies within us. This capacity breaks down into five natural abilities that we all have—to feel, to communicate, to tell the truth, to understand ourselves, and to play. Many men lead fulfilling lives simply because they're aware of this and know how to use these abilities. Ordinarily we develop a capacity for fulfillment during boyhood under the watchful eyes of supportive parents.

Other men with these same abilities lead unfulfilled lives because they don't know about or can't access them. Many had boyhood dreams for a happy future, but conditions at home didn't favor developing or improving much of anything. Still, many men keep trying, developing coping skills to deal with adult conflicts while remaining relatively clueless about how to improve their life.

Now I know that most men prefer a quick answer, a fast way out. "Just tell me what the hell to do and I'll do it!" you may say. Well, sorry, but it's not going to happen. Demanding that others give you an easy way out, or quick answers to your misery, simply doesn't work. It never did, never will. Getting what you want takes work—hard work. And in this case, achieving personal fulfillment means having your innate abilities ready to go to work for you every day.

So, if you continue reading, be prepared to work hard—thinking, learning, reflecting, feeling, imagining, and doing the written exercises suggested in this book. Some of this work is enjoyable, especially the part that involves developing your imagination. I call it "OJT" for on-the-job-training and assume this book's material is new to you, or at least different. Since emotional, thought-provoking work is hard to remember, you're advised at several points to keep progress notes.

The goal of all this work is to rebuild connections to your five natural abilities that have always been available to you but, for whatever reason, became detached from your daily life. But before you can rebuild, you have to clear away the debris that blocks your way. Like any other job, you will get out of it what you put in. Here, the reward for hard work is feeling more fulfilled and being a better partner.

So the basic job is this: finding your way to rebuild connections to your five innate abilities through educating yourself, doing OJT exercises, and sorting through the methods presented in this book and selecting those that best fit your needs. You can then customize these methods for use later when you're done reading. Remember, in OJT, we learn as we go, so be patient and don't expect immediate results.

Below I describe some of the ideas and equipment that you will need along the way.

JOB DESCRIPTION

To do the best job possible in attaining personal fulfillment, it's important to first understand how a boy loses his capacity for fulfillment. This lowers the risk of repeating old patterns and old mistakes, and we're especially vulnerable to doing this under emotional stress. So we'll be looking at

- possible causes for the original emotional disconnection in your family
- the benefits of understanding your history

- how your history continues to affect your daily interactions
- bridge-building equipment; how it works and its limits (take relief in knowing you already have the necessary equipment)

THE BLUEPRINT

A blueprint is a plan or method of imparting knowledge. Other self-improvement blueprints may describe approaches to problem solving through better communication, anger management, healing from infidelity, or dealing with mistrust. This book's bridge-building blueprint helps you develop understanding into the following:

- how you got to be the man you are today
- what you can and cannot give to others
- what you want and don't want in relationships
- what gets in the way of you being content
- what you can do every day to feel fulfilled despite your circumstance

OUR BUILDING CODE

The ideas behind self-improvement books typically evolve from a particular clinical theory or model—or building code. For instance, you may be familiar with the terms cognitive, cognitive-behavioral, behavioral, or "self" psychologies. These are the various building codes used by other authors.

The main building code I use is relational therapy, a clinical theory that stresses the continuing impact of your history on your life today. According to this code, whether your boyhood family was loving or cruel, you will unknowingly shape your current life and relationships so that the here-and-now feels like the there-and-then. You might wonder "Why would I do that? Life wasn't good back then," and you'd be asking an important question. Let's look at why this happens so you'll see the value in doing this book's hard work.

By about age five, each of us inherited from our parents how they felt about relationships. This inheritance was passed down through their family generations, and we had no choice but to accept this. We weren't capable of challenging them and we imagined that if we rejected this inheritance we would defy the bond between them and us (Hedges, in press). So, we took in their patterns of relating even if we silently disagreed. From then on, we felt how they felt about relationships, and we still feel it. Like a family heirloom, we unknowingly honor them by keeping their ways of relating, and how we felt as boys, alive in our adult relationships. This is how our boyhood inheritance—the way our parents felt about each other and about us—became our roadmap for all our future relationships. Whether this meant shaping our adult relationships to be loving or cruel, we've used our roadmap to feel like we felt as a boy. The fear of defying our emotional family bond drives us to do this. Most of us who stop and think about this but then continue anyway do so to avoid feeling guilty about dishonoring our parents. This roadmap is permanent, just like our fingerprints are permanently imprinted into our fingertips.

So, like a traffic engineer, with our roadmap, we try to control the speed with which we give love and attention and in doing so try to direct how others will feel and act toward us. We set up emotional traffic signals so others meet our relational needs—to go ahead, to stop or to proceed with caution. If people obey the rules of our roadway, we not only honor our parents' emotional legacy, we imagine that we heal our boyhood pain of feeling lost or discarded or unloved. If others disobey the rules of our roadway, like a traffic cop, we give them a ticket, and they pay a hefty fine—feeling our anger or our rejection or our coercion.

Conflict in relationships often happens because everyone else inherits relationship roadmaps from their parents, and they're doing what we're doing—trying to get us to follow their roadmap!

For example, consider what happens to a boy growing up in a family where conflict and emotional pain are the norm. According to our building code, the boy inherits his family's relationship patterns of anger, sadness, and fear. By about age five, feeling this way becomes his roadmap for all his future relationships. When he's an adult, he probably won't know about his roadmap (unless he works with a therapist or does some self-improvement work), but he'll follow it nevertheless. And he'll fight with, or he may leave, those who won't comply.

Despite getting love from his partner or his friends or his children, this man is likely to imagine he'll be hurt in these relationships unless he changes them to fit his roadmap. He unknowingly will try to reshape how others interact with him and how they feel about him, so he can feel his life is "on track." Of course, others are using their own roadmaps too, and they won't always comply with his demands or manipulations. Regardless, he'll still achieve his goal of feeling like he did as a boy—disliked, sad, and angry.

Not many of us want to live like this. In order to feel fulfilled, we must stop trying to change our here-and-now so that it replicates our there-and-then. We must learn to respect that others have roadmaps and that they too feel compelled to use them. This is what reading this book will help you do. When you're finished, you'll still have your roadmap, but you'll realize that there's room for, and a need for, mixing other roadmaps with yours. You'll learn about every twist and turn in your roadmap, you'll know it like you know your way home, and you'll have the opportunity to learn about, and to navigate, your partner's roadmap too.

In summary, this building code helps you

- clarify how you keep your family-of-origin environment (that is, your personal history) alive, and how this can help or hinder your personal fulfillment
- recognize when you're using boyhood patterns and know what to do instead
- understand why you fight, get angry, shut people out, and much more
- realize that, just like you, every minute of every day, your partner and your friends and your coworkers use their roadmaps too
- feel more fulfilled, one day at a time

Now, let's look at the equipment you have to do this hard work.

EQUIPMENT

Each of us is born with natural emotional energy. This energy equips us with an emotional responsiveness—it drives us to feel our feelings, desire relationships and it gives us the passion to love and hate. It gives us mental energy to imagine, to think, to understand, to play, and to communicate. In short, this energy equips us with the capacity for personal fulfillment. (You can think of this energy as an internal battery that never runs out of power.) For our purposes, this energy is the only piece of equipment you'll need for this book's OJT.

POURING THE FOUNDATION

On a recent trip to New York City, I crossed the Brooklyn Bridge into lower Manhattan. The view of the city from here is incredible, and as I was admiring the skyline, I realized after a while that I hadn't been thinking at all about what was allowing me to enjoy the view.

I lost track of where I was and kept looking at everything but the bridge I was on. Of course, I knew it was there. Indeed, the bridge is a massive structure that has always amazed me. But at the time, I wasn't thinking about how it contributed to my experience. Later, looking at the photos I took, it dawned on me how often I do this. I can lose sight of what's supporting me in life and allowing me to do what I'm doing, unless I continue with self-improvement work.

Before you can achieve better relationships, you first need greater awareness about your life's foundation. Being a better partner, coworker, and community member requires a working knowledge of your history, since you still carry your history with you. So a big part of the job ahead of you is building a working knowledge of your history's lasting effects, or bridging "then" and "now." You might be thinking "It's useless to dwell on the past," and you'd be right. But thinking about your history in order to self-improve is different from dwelling on the past. If you still believe that your history is unimportant, you may want to skip ahead to read chapter 3. Then, return here, and continue reading.

Doing the exercises in this book, answering the questionnaires, and thinking and reflecting on what you've learned will imbue your history with life, meaning and value. When you connect the there-and-then to the here-and-now, you pour your bridge foundation.

REINFORCEMENT

You will need to reinforce the foundation of your work through keeping progress reports, or notes. Think of how steel rods reinforce concrete and imagine that recording your reactions has a similar effect. Each progress note is another steel rod in the bridge foundation.

Progress notes allow dormant thoughts and unfelt feelings room for expression; they make an idea come to life and a problem less threatening. So, begin with making several progress notes before deciding not to use them as one of your building methods. Several other authors (Jacobs, 2004; McKay & Sutker, 2005; Pennebaker, 2004) attest to this method's effectiveness.

To show how progress notes work, later in this chapter you'll read about my client Graham who, through his progress notes written over roughly one year, realized what was driving him to self-destruct with drugs and alcohol. Remember, each time you press the pen against the paper, changes in your life gain traction.

EQUIPMENT GUIDELINES

Your emotional energy, or your emotional responsiveness, comes from the two parts of your mind: the conscious mind that you're using now, and the unconscious mind that dreams at night, daydreams while you're awake, remembers, makes slips of the tongue, and produces experiences seemingly out of the blue, like a sudden sinking feeling in your stomach. The conscious and unconscious coexist, but understanding how they work together may require some imagination.

Consider the sky. During the day, you don't think about the stars, or the darkness of the universe beyond the daylight, but you know it's there, right? During the day, both daylight and the nighttime sky are there, but you experience them differently.

While you're awake, your conscious and unconscious mind are both active, yet they're working differently. The conscious mind is what you use to think and live your daily life. When you're asleep, your conscious mind rests, while your unconscious mind continues working. In fact, it never stops working.

For example, your unconscious mind deals with, or dreams about, topics too difficult for your conscious mind to manage, like wishes, fantasies, fears, unfelt feelings, and unresolved conflicts. During the day, it stores all your experiences, and by "experience," I mean both what happened and how you felt about it at the time. So getting familiar with what's in your unconscious, especially what affects you today, is important.

Each of us had thousands of family experiences when we were very young boys. This is what I call the *there-and-then* of life. Now imagine that when we were each about five years old, an important event took place in one part of our unconscious storage area. This part, called "My Family History," containing all our family experiences, ran out of space. In other words, during roughly the first five years of life, your unconscious mind stored all your early family relations and how you felt about them—thousands and thousands of times—and then stopped storing any more.

According to this book's building code, the unconscious mind guides us (that is, provides the emotional energy) when we think about ourselves or build relationships. It is constantly reconnecting (bridging) the here-and-now with the there-and-then, especially when we think of ourselves in important relationships. If close connections in the family were lacking or nonexistent, this affects how we think about ourselves and our chance of success in relationships today.

Whether good or bad, early family experience guides our emotional responses now. The there-and-then directs how we use our emotional energy today in intimate relations, and influences our self-criticism or high personal regard. Our unconscious mind can cause us to feel like we're back at home, by associating an emotionally charged adult event with a boyhood event that was similarly emotionally charged. (This idea will be explored in greater detail in following chapters.)

What happened to us when we were small boys cannot change, but we can talk and write about how we felt then and how we continue to feel today. We can start freeing ourselves of old emotional pain; we can stop using behavior patterns that no longer work, and in this way we can stop hurting those who love us.

Building a foundation of awareness requires knowing the impact of history and putting this knowledge to use. You'll use your conscious and unconscious mind, plus some courage, in exploring your history and writing down what's happening to you now.

TESTING A SCALE MODEL

Bridge construction begins with a small-scale model to test the basic design, so let's do something similar. (There are many bridge designs and you might already have one in mind. Good. This means your imagination is at work. If you don't have a picture yet, don't worry; you'll have plenty of opportunities to use your imagination in the following chapters.) The following example applies the ideas discussed so far and introduces the well-known technique called guided imagery.

THE WALKWAY

Imagine two high-rise office buildings, one directly opposite the other with a street between them. A covered walkway connects the buildings at the third or fourth floor. You're standing on one end of the walkway, in the building that's been in use for several years. The other building has recently opened, and you've heard a lot about the interior design, so you decide to use the walkway and visit.

Now, imagine that the end of the walkway where you're standing represents your conscious mind. A few feet away from where you're standing, a sign reads "Leaving Here-and-Now." And looking down to the opposite end of the walkway, you see another sign that reads

"Entrance to There-and-Then." Imagine that by walking across the walkway, you'll walk into your unconscious mind.

You're curious about who's working in the other building and what's going on, and you're eager to meet people on a particular floor of this building, the one called "My Family History." You start to step out onto the walkway, you look down, and you see that there's no floor!

There's only a single cable spanning the two buildings; either you'd have to be a tightrope walker or you'd have to hang upside-down like a monkey using your hands and legs to reach the other side. Impossible you think.

Yet, you still want to get across, so you realize you'll have to build the floor yourself. You'll have to build the walkway that spans from here-and-now to there-and-then using the only equipment you have, your emotionally energy, plus your imagination and courage, since you haven't done this before.

You keep in mind the building code and know that you have the necessary equipment. You remember that self-improvement happens while you do the work. As you work and learn, you see the walkway taking shape, piece by piece. After doing enough work and writing your progress, the walkway is strong enough to support you as you move back and forth between "then" and "now." Your progress notes provide reinforcement. You remember that in any OJT experience, you get out what you put into it; how elaborate and strong your walkway becomes depends on your patience and effort.

GETTING STARTED

At the start of self-improvement work, your bridge is like the walkway between the two buildings that simply isn't there. All many of us have to start with is a single rope that allows our there-and-then to trickle into the here-and-now, like a drop of water making its way down a string. Your bridge building may not need to begin from scratch if you've already done some of this work. In that case, you'll know when to skim through or skip a section or two as you read along. If you are a beginner, however, you'll be building on this idea of a single rope, and you'll reinforce it so that it can carry more and more traffic: your thoughts, feelings, and reactions.

Realize that it's not what's occurring today that keeps you stuck in useless relationships or life patterns. Rather, it's the impact of the there-and-then that can stop you dead in your tracks.

When we become attached to someone in the here-and-now, our there-and-then slowly, and usually without us knowing it, moves into our life, like an invisible roommate. For example, we begin to like someone, and early feelings we had as a kid, like when we thought people cared, stir in our unconscious mind. Old expectations start to move slowly into our conscious mind, and this old way of feeling now becomes what we expect. The old becomes the new.

If we felt unimportant to our parents, today we'd naturally (and unconsciously) be suspicious that our partner does not truly value us. We'd still expect the old outcome, and if it doesn't happen, many of us unknowingly will make it happen. Again, the urge to do this is a natural effort to either re-create how we felt at home or to finish fighting an old family battle. Incidentally, our partners do the same. This is why they fight back, and they too can start an argument seemingly out of nowhere.

Doing self-improvement work helps us develop the skill to quickly realize what is happening in situations like this. Through this book's OJT, you'll learn how you can grow, personally and relationally, from good and bad experiences, and from spending time feeling your emotions while they happen. Every time you sit with your feelings and let them sink in, you move closer to personal fulfillment.

THE PATH TO PROGRESS

Bridge building happens gradually in a series of imaginary journeys between the there-and-then and the here-and-now. You'll get to see this happen using your mind's eye, your natural ability to picture people and scenes in your mind. (Remember the experience of imagining the walkway between the two buildings and standing at one end?) Chapter 3 will expand on the benefits of intentionally traveling to the other "end" of your bridge and exploring what's in your there-and-then.

PAVING THE ROADWAY

Sometimes when you're thinking about a particular person or event, an image of someone else shows up or you have an unexpected bodily sensation, such as a chill, a body ache or pain or numbness, sexual arousal, dizziness, a sudden headache, or unexplained nausea. When these happen, a connection has formed between your there-and-then and your here-and-now, and you've either seen this connection with your mind's eye, or your body felt it. In other words, your unconscious mind has moved an old experience out of storage into your conscious mind.

These other pictures, or random thoughts or bodily sensations, are connections called *associations*. And they're natural. What may surprise you is the important role these associations continue to play in your life—at home, at work, and in the community.

Associations happen when, for example, you close your eyes and listen to music or someone's voice on a CD that guides you to relax. When you associate, your conscious and unconscious minds are both at work, and it's not unusual for your emotional energy to vary from high to low. Your mind normally and automatically connects to, or associates with other seemingly unrelated people, events, feelings, or sensations, and the emotions you have about them can begin to stir. With OJT you'll learn that when you sit with your associations and your reactions to them you'll feel more fulfilled afterward.

Keep in mind that this normally happens several hundred times a day automatically, and we seldom if ever realize it. Like an inaccessible office building, our unconscious mind is a storehouse of early life experiences, especially our early feelings. And we naturally and continually connect old feelings with our current circumstance when what's happening now is emotionally similar to early family life.

When thoughts and feelings that you had as a boy went unexpressed, they live on, and if today's emotional experience is similar, connections to your history are likely to occur. This explains the power in unexpressed feelings from years ago—they're like emotional ghosts that continue to haunt us throughout life. And these are not always the Casper the Friendly Ghost variety.

Each time you travel into your there-and-then and realize what patterns are ineffective, like your rage, the pattern loses its impact. For example, you might stop your pattern of getting angry for no apparent reason. And as you do the exercises in this book, you'll make repeated associations like this and build a bridge that's open for thoughts and feelings to move across.

You'll see into your there-and-then with your mind's eye, and you won't have much control over what your mind associates to. But don't worry about this; it's normal. And don't worry about feeling overloaded with too much information when doing the exercises. Your brain typically regulates how much information moves back and forth between its parts.

Through these connections or associations, parts of your history that have unknowingly but relentlessly affected your life will become clearer. If you already know what gets in your way, like an addiction or anger, you'll now think about these problems differently and will be better able to do something to improve how your life feels.

You'll learn much more about how, why, and when your life and relationships don't work. To start, all you'll need to do is picture something today that doesn't work, then let your mind's eye see if something from your boyhood is being reenacted, like an old battle with mom or dad, and then write down your reactions. Doing this enough times will reduce the impact of this piece of there-and-then in your life today.

A historical note: Our building code of relational therapy has its basis in the work of Sigmund Freud. About one hundred years ago, Freud realized that people changed for the better simply by saying whatever came to mind in the counseling room. This became known as the "fundamental rule" in psychoanalysis (Greenson, 1967, p.10). In so doing, he helped his clients build a bridge between their history and their present lives. He simply provided an environment in which people could talk about whatever came to mind and he would clarify for them the connections between "then" and "now." This was a freeing experience and with repeated associations and clarifications, in time his clients' problems were resolved. Currently, the "fundamental rule" is commonly referred to as "free association," and you will learn more about this in the chapters that follow.

THE PAYCHECK

You'll receive a big reward for doing this work—immediate improvements you'll see and feel in your life and in your relationships. Inside the pay envelope are self-improvement methods usable for as long you need, to build better relationships and feel more fulfilled. Think of this as a stream of passive income since this payoff lasts a long time. Graham's effort at bridge building is a good example of how OJT works. You'll read more about Graham in later chapters.

GRAHAM'S STORY

Graham entered therapy soon after his arrest for driving while intoxicated. He was 44 years old. He's been working on himself for a year now, using the same tools that this book will teach you how to use.

Initially, Graham talked of a pervasive feeling of emptiness despite his financial success in his career as an architect. For some years, he'd been randomly misusing drugs and alcohol, and he couldn't understand what triggered this need to "numb out," as he called it. While not a daily drinker or drug user, he described random, strong impulses to drink or get high. Despite having had several close relationships, he'd never married, always living alone.

He described his boyhood family environment without much emotion, and it was clear that any sense of connection to his parents or to his two older brothers was almost nonexistent. He described his mother as being "a good housekeeper, a good cook." She took him and his two brothers to school, church, and to sporting events. But he felt a chill each time he would talk about her.

He described his father as a "good provider," a hardworking construction worker, and a quiet man, except when "he'd drink the weekend away." His father ruled the house with intimidation. When he was sober, Graham said, his glare was enough to scare anyone into doing what he wanted.

Graham described the fighting between his parents as "drunken shoving matches": they'd scream at each other and threaten to leave, but neither was ever hurt physically. When Graham was four years old, his parents divorced. He and his brothers went to live with different relatives in neighboring towns for the next three years. His father would visit each son twice a month, but Graham didn't see his mother during this time or his brothers. He later learned that his mother had remarried during the separation and had given birth to another son.

In an early session, Graham talked of an image in which a boy stood at his aunt's front door peering over his suitcase. He watched the taxicab pull away and saw the back of his mother's head as she checked her makeup in a hand mirror. With blank expression, he described how this image still affected his mood, how his anger "sometimes feels like a car-crash in slow motion."

During this time away from his family, Graham discovered that good grades in school paid off. Over time, he became an intelligent, detached boy, well-liked by teachers and relatives, but often he felt like a burden. He described himself as a boy who felt ashamed for simply being alive.

Graham's parents eventually remarried, and the boys returned home. Graham described in great detail the cold reception from his mother, who seemed preoccupied with her newest son. He never forgot her remark: "Wipe your dirty feet before you come in!" At age seven, life in the home returned to "normal," only now both parents were heavy drinkers and the random screaming matches returned. The boys learned to hide.

Graham wasn't sure at what point he became suspicious of other people, only that it began soon after his return home. He recollected receiving compliments from teachers that he never believed. At age 44, professional and social acknowledgment still brought the same internal response: "What's the real agenda here...what's she or he after?" He'd grow suspicious when a woman smiled at him and could vividly describe his association: "Since I was a boy, women's smiles always reminded me of a long shiny sword sliding from its sheath." As treatment progressed, he realized the connection between the sword and his mother's seductive smile, her way of getting men to do her bidding.

In therapy, Graham realized his history had value—that knowing it could help his recovery and healing. With each guided imagery exercise, he could see a connection between the boy and the adult. By keeping progress notes after these exercises, he's come to understand where his random pain and urges to drink come from.

Initially, keeping progress notes was hard, until he understood his resistance to documenting family pain. After a year of bridge building, Graham knows he is not *in* these early scenes that his mind's eye sees. He now lets the image happen, using the acceptance and separation tools covered in chapter 2. He describes this as "watching the airport baggage claim conveyor carry my family, and my old feelings in and out of my life. I know which bags to pick up and which ones not to." He still feels suspicious when he meets new people, but he's quick to sort out what belongs where.

He's accepted that these reactions are part of his "living record" (Hedges, 1994, p 5). Like an imaginary internal CD player containing all his associations, early scenes of getting angry at those who tried to comfort him during his time away from the family continue showing up in his mind's eye. Only now, he's more prepared, especially for reactions that seemingly come out of the blue. He can accept these imaginary connections for what they are, he knows what to expect, and uses his bridge to recognize boyhood feelings of being trapped, or alone, or suspicious.

He now describes his bridge as "fireproof, loaded with expansion joints, shock absorbers, and thick pavement," which he understands comes from having made hundreds of associations, keeping progress notes, and using the self-improvement tools that work best for him.

Graham still fights random urges to drink and has "drinking" dreams. He'll wake in a cold sweat, terrified for a few seconds that he's taken another drink or had another line of cocaine. But he's quicker to recognize the association of being fourteen and to his father's threat to slice off his hands if Graham ever drank again. At random times, he'll feel profound grief and emptiness washing over him, like an ocean wave. But he knows the benefit of sitting with his feelings and that every time he feels the boy's pain, a bit more of it leaves him, creating space in him for the boy's aliveness and for more adult fulfillment.

Despite all he now knows, Graham is still drawn to unavailable women, who remind him of his mother. He recognizes that the urge to go home is powerful. But these feelings no longer drive him to drink.

WHAT'S NEXT FOR YOU

No matter how much self-study you do, your unconscious mind will continue to make associations. But like Graham, you can learn to connect today's reactions (like anger, confusion, or the need for a drink) to how you felt and reacted when you were younger. And you won't have to morph yourself into someone else, change your personality, or spend years in therapy to do it. But you must do some work.

You may privately shed a tear as you read ahead or as you do the exercises and reflect on your life. But trust me, it's your old pain crossing your bridge into the here-and-now, and by understanding this, talking about it and keeping progress notes, the pain losses its stranglehold on your personal fulfillment.

In time, you'll stop picking the same partner again and again. You won't hurt so bad that you need a drink or have a need to use porn. You'll realize the devastating effects of infidelity or working at a career you despise. Each time you connect "then" and "now," you'll think about the boy, feel the old feelings pass through, like Graham's conveyor belt, and feel more fulfilled.

You'll be able to work through fears of intimacy that you might have. For example, you'll be better equipped to deal with feeling abandoned, and you'll understand why you get angry if you have to wait longer than you planned to or if someone doesn't return your phone call on time. You'll stop demanding that friends and family read your mind, and you'll realize that others are not in your life merely to meet your needs.

You'll be able to sit with your partner while he or she struggles with feelings, and you won't jump to conclusions or try to "fix" their situation. You'll do all you can to understand your partner, to consider their perspective and to see yourself the way your partner sees you. You'll be able to sit with your feelings and you'll grow more fulfilled, because you'll make the time to feel your feelings, whether they're good or bad. You'll do this instead of shutting off your feelings with alcohol, drugs, pornography, infidelity or overworking.

These are just some of the possibilities available to you from doing this book's OJT. But before you begin your journey into the there-and-then, let's look at some well-known obstacles that can interfere with your hard work.

Chapter 2
Construction Delays

When you want to improve your life, part of your psychological makeup can work against you. This is known as *resistance*. Most of us have several ways of resisting change. Generally, resistance and self-improvement go together. Often showing up during self-improvement work as unexpected thoughts or feelings, resistance doesn't mean you won't or can't change, but it can slow you down or stop you.

Here is one form that resistance to self-improvement commonly takes:

- "I already know this stuff about myself."
- "It couldn't have been *that* bad."
- "This is ridiculous!"
- "Men aren't supposed to *feel*."
- "Well, of *course* I was angry about that!"
- "My life wasn't important; there's no use in thinking about it."

What you're doing here is talking yourself out of trying. But resistance can also take less obvious forms, such as becoming bored or hungry, starting to daydream or get sleepy, when you think about emotional situations from your boyhood or in your adult life.

Why and how resistance happens will become clearer in later chapters. At this point, it's important to know that it does happen, to recognize when it's happening, and to know what you can do about it.

Circle anything in the following list that you have noticed yourself doing when you think about emotional situations:

- forgetting
- losing focus
- daydreaming
- getting drowsy
- getting bored
- becoming restless
- getting hungry
- getting angry
- going "blank"
- drinking

If you have other responses that weren't on this list, write about them in your progress notes.

As you proceed through this book, you may find that you have certain reactions to doing self-improvement work. You may find yourself doing the following:

- being unable to remember your personal history
- writing about but having no reaction to your history
- hiding self-improvement work from others
- feeling ashamed about your history, so you don't think or write about it
- talking your way out of trying
- intellectualizing about rather than experiencing emotional pain

If you encounter these or any other forms of resistance as you do any of the exercises in this book, you can begin to deal with them by taking the following steps:

1. Pause. Put the book down.
2. Focus on the resistance. For example, ask yourself, "How long have I felt this way?" Your mind's eye will begin connecting to other thoughts and feelings from your history.
3. Write about these connections in your progress notes. Include your feelings, thoughts, and any body sensations.
4. Breathe deeply a few times, relax, and restart the exercise.
5. If you still have a hard time, skip the exercise. Keep reading and do the exercises that follow. You can always return to any exercise.
6. If necessary, refer to the websites mentioned in the introduction to help you reduce anxiety.

OVERCOMING RESISTANCE: ACCEPTANCE AND SEPARATION

Two effective tools for dealing with unexpected emotional reactions are *acceptance* and *separation*. Other self-improvement books show how you can use acceptance and separation to cope with anxiety, worry, and anger. The following sections focus on how you can use these tools to cope with resistance to doing OJT work.

ACCEPTANCE

Acceptance is recognizing when hurtful feelings or thoughts belong to history and then "making space for them—without acting on them."(Eifert, McKay & Forsyth, 2006, p. 7). Say you encounter unexpected fear during an OJT exercise. There are two ways of looking at your fear. You can say to yourself:

1. *"It's frightening to think about."*
2. *"I was frightened as a boy."*

In the first instance, you're still afraid, still viewing history "from" the fear (Brantley, 2007, p. 25), and you remain afraid. This is a form of "cognitive fusion" (Lejune, 2007, p. 23), or the "fusion" of your thought of the boy's fear with actually being afraid. Here's how you can begin to accept your fear so that it will no longer slow you down.

Again, when you experience unexpected fear, you would pause and put the book aside. Next, you would let your mind's eye see the scared boy, and you would begin realizing the boy's fear was a necessary safeguard at the time. But now, you the adult no longer need the boy's fear. Thinking this way, while you imagine the boy and write about it in your progress notes, helps prevent you from fusing with the boy's experience. You're able to picture the boy when he was afraid, and not risk becoming afraid. Now you'll understand why he was afraid instead of feeling it now. Your feelings from the past can move freely into the here-and-now, and the traffic along your bridge won't be delayed.

Through acceptance, you can be caring and respectful of yourself. When, for example, you accept that the boy's fear protected him, you won't think, "I must've been a real coward, a real jerk, to let that happen." You'll accept that fear was part of your history "without judging or getting all tangled up" in it again (Eifert, et al. 2006, p. 100).

SEPARATION

Separation, or getting some distance or perspective, is the tool that allows you to say "I was frightened as a boy, but I don't have to feel afraid now." Managing unexpected reactions this way is like watching a movie. For example, according to Chad Lejune (2007, p. 85), "Your worries are much like the images on the [movie] screen. By sitting back and observing them as just one part of your experience, your relationship to them changes. Like the person who is only half-watching the movie, it becomes less important what specific images happen to be on the screen at any given time."

You can use separation as a tool to handle unexpected feelings. Say you are writing progress notes about your fear as a little boy. Then suddenly you feel bitter and have the urge to drink. In the same way you'd watch an instant replay, you can use your mind's eye to imagine a movie screen with the little boy as the "star." Like a movie theater, you can watch from a distance as the boy feels the bitterness. And with instant replay, you can watch this as many times as you need to see what really happened to him. In this way you're separated from the unexpected reaction of bitterness, and there's no need to submerge your pain in alcohol.

In Graham's case, when he meets new people, he's now aware of two choices. He can become mistrustful and let his suspicion characterize who he is, or he can accept and step away from the fear that's underneath his mistrust. Again, doing this is "making space for" the fear (Eifert, et al. p. 7). Graham can then imagine the fearful boy and assure him that he won't be abandoned, or, rather, Graham is reassured that he has the capacity to tolerate abandonment.

Think of yourself like a boxer in the ring, ducking and weaving around the "ring of life," trying to protect yourself from the unexpected punch of emotions. And like a boxer who wants to win and knows he'll probably get hurt trying, when you feel yourself slowing down or wanting to stop, push yourself to stay in the ring a little longer and think about your resistance. Are you afraid of change? What do you gain from *not* changing?

There's no referee in the ring of life, and you're not shadow boxing. Like the boxer who wants to win, the only way I know to deal with resistance and unexpected emotions is hard work. Thirty years after my last drink, I know that being an addict will never change. But I do know that accepting and separating from the boy's pain prepares me to cope with my random urges to drink.

Chapter 3
Time Travel and the Value of History

In this chapter, you will learn more about how the unconscious and the conscious mind work together. This will require that you keep using your imagination. Like being in a dream, you can't actually use logic to figure out what you will be reading about. For example, you'll read about make-believe vehicles bringing passengers from your history into the here-and-now. You'll be asked to picture this, and even more, as you read, you'll be asked to build an imaginary bridge from *then* to *now*. Outside the realm of psychology, this way of learning may make little sense. In OJT, it is intentional, for having a better life, and better relationships requires you to create a good outcome, in your mind, beforehand.

You will learn about your history's inevitable arrival in the here-and-now and how this is not the same as "living in the past." You will understand that your boyhood still has value and meaning, and that knowing this can help you stop doing what doesn't work. You'll also begin learning about the "boy," which is a metaphor for the part of you that continues to carry your boyhood emotional experiences. You will begin to imagine this boy as the "ambassador" of your history, and imagining this boy will be important to all your continued self-improvement work. By the end of this chapter you will understand yourself better, your imagination will almost be at "full throttle," and your bridge building will be well underway.

Let's pause here and learn about a simple exercise you can do when you're not reading. Remember that your unconscious mind is always active, right? It's also good to know that your conscious imagination and your unconscious mind work together, like a piano player's hands. They work separately and together at the same time. In a similar way, in OJT, you can use your unconscious mind and your conscious imagination, while you're awake, anytime you choose. This is called "free association," the idea introduced by Sigmund Freud about one hundred years ago.

EXERCISE: FREE ASSOCIATION

Find a quiet place. Indoors or outdoors will do, but make sure that you are in a relaxing space where you won't be distracted by work or household tasks or other people. While sitting or lying down, close your eyes, and then let your thoughts happen. When you leave your thoughts alone, without trying to make sense of them, you are freely associating. One thought may seem totally unrelated to the one you just had, and from the next one you're about to have. Do this exercise for about five to ten minutes.

Afterwards, write down some of the thoughts that went through your mind and what you were feeling. For example, what did you think about? What images did you see? Did your mind dart from one thought to another? Did you laugh? Were you sad or anxious? Don't worry if you can't remember everything that you just thought about, or how you felt. The point is to notice that you have thoughts and feelings that seem unrelated to each other or that have no logical connection.

This exercise helps you begin to explore parts of yourself that you may have always known about but haven't spent much time thinking about (Bollas, 1987, pp. 3-4). For instance, you can begin to understand the things you've "put behind you" that still affect you. This builds self-awareness, and you can do it anytime. You will use free association in upcoming chapters, and you will use it to learn more about what's stored in your there-and-then.

Many men live by the motto of "just put it behind you and move on." This motto reflects a typical male pattern of dealing with feelings. As men, we're not supposed to have feelings, because when we were boys, expressing or trying to understand our feelings was discouraged. Still, we had them. So, now, as adults, when we move or change jobs or fail at a new business or have dreams smashed by tragedy or lose a relationship, we may think "putting it behind me" works. Perhaps it does for a while. But eventually, we get weary from dragging a wagonload of unfelt experiences. Some men get depressed, and then they put this into their wagon too, adding even more emotional weight to their lives.

Freely associating helps empty the wagon. The feelings you've "put behind" since boyhood can now be thought about and expressed, and you can spend time sitting in these feelings and improve your self-understanding. And the value in keeping progress notes during or after this exercise cannot be overstated. The things you write may fascinate you (it can feel like you're in a dream) and can help you begin thinking and feeling better about yourself.

Now, it's time to get back to on-the-job training (OJT). It's time to learn more about how the there-and-then (the content of your unconscious mind) impacts your personal fulfillment and how you can access it to understand old patterns.

THE TRAFFIC

Boyhood experiences move into the present at different speeds, sometimes arriving on cue and sometimes arriving out of the blue.

Picture a fleet of make-believe taxicabs, owned and operated by the Experience Transit Agency, and imagine that this agency is responsible for transporting all your boyhood experiences, back and forth, between your conscious mind and the there-and-then. Imagine taxis moving single file, gradually bringing boyhood experiences into your awareness, and that this is how you "begin to remember." Imagine too, that some experiences gather into small groups after they arrive. This happens, for example, when you recall a series of events together, like "Now I remember that! And then I remember this happened, then that happened."

Now let's look at another way the Experience Transit Agency handles your experiences. Picture a high-speed bullet train that, like the taxicab, brings one passenger, or one early experience, into the here-and-now. The only difference is that this happens fast. This happens, for instance, when you have out-of-the-blue thoughts or feelings, or have images suddenly come to mind.

Imagine too that each taxicab or train passenger carries a suitcase, and that inside this suitcase is a neatly packed piece of your history. This piece of history is unpacked in the here-and-now, and then you feel the old feeling or think the old thought.

ARRIVALS AND DEPARTURES

The taxicabs arrive on cue. Picture two busy transportation hubs, one in the there-and-then and the other in the here-and-now. At each end of your bridge (the one you're building as you think about it), hundreds of your passengers depart and arrive every day. Most of these passengers wait patiently for taxicabs, each carrying a suitcase and its precious contents.

At the departure point, taxicabs wait at the curb single file, with signs in their windows identifying the boyhood experience that's needed next in the here-and-now. Each time *now* feels like *then* in your adult life, one or more of these imaginary taxis arrives in your conscious mind, and you gradually become aware that you're replaying your history.

Other experiences arrive in the here-and-now without warning, aboard the bullet train. (This excludes any experiences that are part of past trauma or bereavement.) Examples of sudden out-of-the-blue events include times you're startled, ashamed, confused, or suddenly angry, or have a craving to drink or use a drug. These are the feelings that have been unpacked in the here-and-now that are giving you clues to unfinished emotional business in your family. Having out-of-the-blue reactions is one of the ways your mind tries to tell you about an underlying emotional struggle.

These fast-moving reactions aren't always easily understood compared to those arriving gradually. Still, you can explore why these happen by using free association exercises, like the one described earlier in this chapter, and by keeping progress notes. Doing this can give you insight into your underlying struggle. Here are some examples of out-of-the-blue experiences. Can you relate to any of the following?

- You get angry for no apparent reason when you see a stranger who resembles your father. You decided years ago to "cut him out of your life." But the boy inside you hasn't been able to do that, so he gets off the bullet train right on the sidewalk where you're standing.
- Normally, telling your kids you're sick, when you're actually hung over, is easy. Lately, when you lie to them, you see yourself as a boy, about age seven. This is your son's age, and the age you were when you began stealing. You thought this part of you was "over and done with." Now, the boy steps off the train and unpacks your shame every time you lie to your children.

- Visits home trigger an urge to drink. You know this will happen, but you refuse to think about why it happens. You only think about the alcohol numbing your pain, which makes the idea of visiting bearable for you. Each time you visit, the boy unpacks the family's emptiness when you walk in the front door.

- You gave yourself extra time, yet you're late for another first date. Each time you meet someone new, the boy takes the bullet train into the here-and-now and unpacks your fear about not belonging in your family. His suitcase weighs enough to slow down your car.

- Each time you lift weights, your mood sours. The little boy doesn't like it when you try to bury him, or his feelings, under all that muscle. The train drops him off at the gym's front door every day you're there.

THE FUEL

Most car engines today generate horsepower by mixing gasoline and a spark, under controlled conditions. Then, the driver puts the car in motion. Many times, when an adult situation is emotionally similar to a boyhood event, this resembles the gasoline and spark in a car's engine. Under the right conditions, this combination results in power and movement. For instance, let's say you receive a gift from someone close, and instead of feeling good, you suddenly feel sad. This reaction confuses you. You want to feel happy but just can't.

The gift giver wants to please you, and you want to reciprocate, like the boy who wanted to please his parents. So, like the boy did, you pretend to be happy, even though you're confused about being sad. All you know is that this scene feels familiar, but, like before, you resist thinking about it. You tell yourself "be a man, just get over it!"

So what happened when you got this gift? The boy unpacked the lingering sadness a small boy felt, while holding an unopened birthday gift and seeing his parents leave to have their own fun.

SPEED LIMITS

One way to picture how your mind works is to imagine taxi riders and train passengers moving freely between your conscious and unconscious mind, at speeds called for by your current situation. Like the examples described earlier in this chapter, some experiences are needed immediately, like those that are out of the blue; others are needed gradually, like those needed when you remember a sequence of events.

During this book's OJT work, traffic can move uninterrupted, but like at a real job site, imaginary traffic may get delayed during an imaginary construction job, like your bridge-building. You've read about some of these delays, or the resistances, in chapter 2. These are the different ways your associations can slow down or stop. Let's look at how and why this resistance happens, so if it happens to you as you are reading this book and doing the exercises, you can get moving again.

Our brain naturally tries to protect us from feeling old emotional pain that we've tried to "put behind us," whether we were actually hurt or we imagined that we were hurt. Stated differently, our brain has different ways to defend us from feeling pain from our history. In psychology, *resistance* and *defenses* are considered natural, and everyone is expected to have them. To illustrate this, consider your OJT work and why you're reading this book.

Why can't you simply tell yourself to be fulfilled and have it happen? One possibility is that you lost the capacity for personal fulfillment when, as a boy, it wasn't okay to be a normal, fun-loving kid. Maybe it was risky. Maybe your parents were so distressed about their lives because of war, or finances, or their own fears from their history, that in their minds everyone had to be miserable, including their children. So, when you were happy, they got angry. Even though it's natural for a boy to feel fulfilled simply by being playful, you had to hold back these urges. You wanted to fit in, and being unhappy was what they needed from you. In other words, you defended yourself against getting punished for feeling fulfilled by isolating, by becoming a "people pleaser" or a "doormat," or by fantasizing that your family was happy. Now, when you read this book about fulfillment, you become drowsy, or you get hungry, or you want a drink, or you get angry at your partner (who gave you this book and asked you to read it).

You can work through traffic delays with the tools in chapter 2, using the websites listed in the introduction, by regularly keeping progress notes and dedicating time to freely associating when you're not reading. Remember, regardless of speed, and despite construction delays, experiences leave your there-and-then hundreds of times each day. Remember also to take one page at a time, take one step at a time, putting one foot in front of the other. Do the work and you'll keep getting good results.

STARTING THE ENGINE

Doing this work will bring your history to life. You may already be recalling more of your boyhood, either when you're awake or when you're dreaming. When you begin connecting "then" and "now," it can feel like you're in the driver's seat of a fast car. You can simultaneously feel excitement, fear, anxiety, even exhilaration, along with being intensely focused. Then problems can begin clearing up, bad patterns can stop, and people will tell you you're "different." Boyhood events, that have had little or no meaning before, become alive. And a life that has meaning also has value. But only you can breathe life into your history. Only you can give it meaning and value (Bollas, 1995).

It's hard to avoid the effects of history. Simply saying something like "the past is the past" won't prevent suitcases of old feelings from unsnapping in the here-and-now. Your need to drink, use drugs, your rage, or your reliance on porn or overworking, don't simply disappear because you tell them to. History seeks expression: the unconscious mind keeps turning the key, trying to start the engine, and either you're in the driver's seat because you've done this OJT work, or you're not. Regardless, history will arrive as naturally as water flows downhill.

TWO DIFFERENT VEHICLES

There is an important distinction between the idea of you "living in the past" and you exploring your history's value and meaning in the here-and-now.

- Living in the Past

Living in the past usually means you've selected a time when life seemed easier or a time you were happier or had less responsibility or were prosperous, or maybe when your luck held out. Now you're like a stage director rearranging props for a play—trying to set up your life so that it resembles "the good old days," all the while hoping you'll feel better.

My new client, Glen, "lives for football." There's nothing bad about this, or having an interest in any sport, until it compensates for feeling miserable. Glen is compulsive about attending, or watching, every game. He knows all the players' stats on every team, in each division. He's constantly talking about playing college ball, being in great shape, being popular, and having lots of girlfriends. He talks as though this was all recent, but in truth, his story took place ten or more years ago. Here's how, and why, he might do this.

Lately, at work, he's had setbacks, and his relationships at home haven't been the best. He doesn't have the tools or skills to deal with emotional situations. Instead, he resists feeling like a failure by recalling a time he was truly happy, and tries to repeat it. Now, when someone tells him what they see, he gets angry and drinks. He relies on one part of his life, a fantasy, to feel better. He does this intentionally and can't understand why this irritates his family and coworkers. Glen lives in the past.

- Reliving History

Associating to the there-and-then is seldom, if ever, something you think of beforehand. It's automatic. The taxicabs know what passengers are needed in the here-and-now. Old patterns and feelings are brought across your bridge each time *now* feels like *then.*

It seems, for most of us, that somewhere in our unconscious mind is the fantasy that the there-and-then was a good place, a place where we were loved and valued by our family. (Remember, this is in our building code.) If we weren't, we pretended it was, and this became our fantasy. And now, in our close relationships, we re-create being at home, and old patterns reappear. Only these no longer work. (Remember the emotional ghosts that aren't the Casper the Friendly Ghost variety?) And since our partner does the same thing, we fight with each other. Once we learn about this, we can stop fighting.

In re-creating history, many times our goal is healing old emotional pain. Think about the guy who says "Whoever I date, it turns out the same way—she leaves me." One likely boyhood experience in this man's history would be that his mother left when he was a boy, and now he clings to women he dates. This man sets up his life today to feel like yesterday; only he doesn't know it. He clings, so "mother" won't leave; only this doesn't work, and he ends up alone, like he was as a boy.

Repeating history also happens when life is good. When we're happy now, our automatic associations reproduce our happy history. If love and care were part of life, we'd likely reproduce it today. Old experiences, good or bad, come to life through associations and continue fueling the taxicabs and the bullet train.

OLD ROADS, NEW ROAD TRIPS

Exploring your history, and recognizing its meaning and value, is similar to repaving an old road. This road's pavement is cracked, with the wreckage of unheard family messages from your history strewn along the sides. Consider these statements; they're what some men believe:

- "She's just like my useless mother. I better get used to it."
- "Getting married will be the same living hell it was for mom and dad."
- "Friends eventually stab you in the back, just like my brothers did."

If you think these thoughts or believe they're true, stop. Take the next exit and get off this old road, and learn why these beliefs and thoughts keep driving you away from personal fulfillment. Each road trip you take to the there-and-then repaves your awareness of what happens to you, why it happens, and when it's likely to happen again. And the road trips begin in chapter 4.

Like learning how to ride a bicycle, at some point the training wheels come off. For you, now is that time. The rest of this book asks you to apply what you've learned in this chapter, using the emotionally energy of your conscious and unconscious mind, so the taxicabs and the bullet train can help you arrive at your destination—personal fulfillment. The remainder of this chapter shows how many communities value and use the idea of history.

<u>VALUE IN HISTORY</u>

This idea, that your history has value and meaning appears in many areas of life. Here are a few examples that affect me. Depending on your history, you may have many others.

- The Grocery Store

When you see a canned or packaged food labeled as "old-fashioned" or using "the original recipe," do you associate these words with the good feeling of sitting among others and sharing a home-cooked meal? If so, these good feelings could influence what you buy.

Is this advertising, in fact, making good use of something we don't typically think about, like how our reliance on everything but a home-cooked meal—micro waving, fast-foods, a dizzying array of protein bars and energy drinks—indeed might be harmful to family relationships? Apart from holiday seasons, the idea of families and friends gathering for a home-cooked family meal is becoming as rare as some antiques.

- Antiques

Have you ever wondered why old furniture, like an old picture frame, and even old trinkets command a high price? Think for a minute about wandering the aisles of an antique show and why you might make a purchase. Here are a few possibilities:

- You're making an investment.
- You admire long-lost craftsmanship and durability.
- You're reminded of times when simplicity and quality were the norm.
- You're reminded of your youth.

Isn't it interesting how many of us feel nostalgic about an old car, or how we yearn for "the way things used to be"? I think of this yearning as displaying that history has value, whether it was a good experience or a bad one, it's still "preserved" (Bollas, 1995, p. 118) in the there-and-then.

Old cars and antiques can bring on powerful associations. While we hold or admire an antique or gaze at an old car, we may begin daydreaming about earlier times when we were (or should've been) cared for. Or maybe we simply daydream about "then" being better than "now." Feelings from history, even some that we may not have felt for many years wash over us like a wave at the shore.

In this way, many relics have emotional value, and some of us will pay a small fortune to recapture the way we felt long ago. And at the antique show or car show, we're vulnerable to these associations. A piece of history climbs aboard the bullet train as we look at, or touch, an old object—the seller, like the train's conductor, invitingly saying, "All aboard!"

- Education

History has more than commercial value in our society. We want our schools to teach the value of our nation's history and to instill in our children a sense of value in world history and their heritage. We encourage our children to learn about others' lives and struggles, as long as the discussion isn't about us.

Why is it that we often discourage discussions of personal history? Why is it preferable to say "I get that from my dad" when we're talking about a positive trait, while it's usually not okay to say "I developed my courage as a boy on my own. I had to. My house was a scary place. We each found our own way; it was like living with roommates." It's acceptable, and even expected of us, to credit our strengths to our knowing someone else, but we seldom talk about relationships that left us damaged. Why is the truth viewed as blaming our parents or us shirking responsibility?

- Employment

Consider the impact of your professional resume or curriculum vitae. These documents describe your professional growth—your career history. And when potential employers try to assess how well you'd fit with their organization, they look at your academic background, employment progression, community affiliations, and your references.

This history describes how you arrived at where you are today, professionally. It also describes how well you've done as a colleague and coworker. Here, as in your personal life, history impacts the future.

Our life takes on new meaning when we talk about it. Our words create our history as we tell others what happened, how we felt, and, more to the point, how history continues to affect us (Bollas, 1995, pp. 103-145). These events started our social, emotional, psychological, and intellectual development. We internalized early patterns of being with others, and this left behind an internal template of how relationships should feel.

This template stays with us throughout life, regardless of what happened, and continues to pattern adult life, including our career, views of intimacy, and choice of partners. And this happens every day in all of our interactions. This is our history, and when we speak of it or write about it, we imbue it with value and meaning. This is why many of us spend quiet hours walking the aisles among antiques and old cars, feeling our history stir inside.

All life experience, good and bad, has meaning and value, not only to us but to those who care about us. When we share our history, we tell others about how we have built a life. When others are aware of us in this way, it helps them understand why we do what we do.

A history that's alive and known allows us to change ineffective patterns, now. We learn how they began, why we've needed to keep them alive, and what we can do instead. History clarifies where we've been; it illuminates our bridge in the darkest of times and helps us find our way to fulfillment.

Now, an update on your OJT progress. Remember the walkway between the two buildings? The walkway wasn't there, but only a single cable, right? At this point, your bridge has more structure and is ready for traffic that will cement your peace of mind. Why? Because you've read this far, you're still reading, and this tells you that your imagination and unconscious mind have been working hard. Good job. This is progress—you've reached a milestone.

SITTING IN HISTORY

In the following chapters, you'll be asked to think about and imagine as far back in your life as you can, to a time your emotional and psychological life began, and this can bring up unexpected reactions.

And you'll be asked to sit with your feelings and your reactions to your history so that you can experience them and make connections to other aspects of your life. This is hard work, but when you're done, you'll begin feeling the fulfillment you're looking for.

For many men, doing this is refreshing. These men feel the burden of their history lifted and be set aside when they sit with feelings that were shut down long ago. The remaining work in this book can be as refreshing for you too. You'll learn how to stop reliving the hurtful aspects of the there-and-then in the here-and-now, and how to set aside the parts of your history that still burden you.

Again, feeling a strong reaction, like anger or anxiety, rarely happens when you read a self-improvement book. Still, when you read this or any other book, it can happen. For some men, especially men who are survivors of boyhood trauma, doing some of this work can stir up uncomfortable thoughts, feelings, or unexpected physical reactions, like a sinking feeling in the gut or a headache. If you have a reaction like this, remember to pause, put the book aside and let the reaction pass. If doing the work in an exercise is a struggle, just read through the exercise without doing the work. If reading the topic continues to upset you, you can skip over it and try reading it later, or choose to not read the topic altogether. To get further help with anxiety, you can also reread chapter 2 or refer to the websites listed in the introduction.

Even if you avoid some of this book's topics, you will have ample opportunity in other chapters to rid yourself of old relationship patterns. In the end, you'll develop the courage to sit with the bad feelings as well as good feelings. The payoff—more personal fulfillment and greater peace of mind—is worth the effort.

Now, let's take a few road trips.

Chapter 4
Road Trips

The human brain builds millions of new electrical pathways from birth to late adolescence. Your brain, like the brain of other men, wasn't finished until your late teens to your early twenties. This is normal brain development.

So, like most boys, you didn't have the brainpower to fully understand why others acted as they did, including your family. You naturally assumed home was normal. You didn't yet have the capacity to fully understand or to analyze events happening around you. But being there, and feeling what you felt about being there, etched itself into your there-and-then. Whether your parents were happy and loving or were cruel and violent, how it felt to be with them and how it felt to be in their environment became your roadmap for future relationships.

Relationships are emotional experiences, not analytical decisions. You don't understand love; it's just there. Furthermore, according to our building code, by the time you were about age five, your roadmap was finished, in terms of how relationships should feel. What you learned then is how you form attachments today.

In this chapter, you'll be asked to do six guided imagery exercises designed to help you revisit parts of your history, and in this way, you'll come to a better understanding of how you feel and think about attachments. These six exercises are imaginary road trips into a part of the unconscious mind where your family history is stored. You can call this storehouse of memory "My Family History." You'll learn how the there-and-then is etched in your mind and how easy it is to explore. You'll be guided toward images of a boy at different ages and learn to view him as the ambassador for that part of your history that you're visiting. You'll move back and forth between then and now, building your bridge and bringing your history back to life. You'll imagine talking with the boy, and you'll uncover his unmet emotional needs and learn how you can help him. You'll understand how these unmet needs relate to your needs today.

If you haven't done guided imagery, it may seem strange at first, but you'll soon discover how this work can instill value and meaning into your family history. If you've done guided imagery work before, you will be familiar with the benefits of these exercises. In my case, when an urge to drink wanders onto my bridge, seemingly out of nowhere, I take a road trip or two, spending time with the boy, and this immediately kills the urge to drink. When you've finished this book, you'll be able to use guided imagery in the same way to cope with your own issues.

Exercise 1 is a warm-up road trip. In exercises 2 to 4, you'll imagine different segments of your history. In exercise 5, you'll imagine being with your parents when they were children. In exercise 6, you'll see how this work can be applied to everyday life. It's best to do the exercises in sequence and to follow the instructions. All you'll need is your imagination, a pen, some paper, and a place where you won't be disturbed. There are several ways to do each exercise. You may want to record the exercise instructions so that you can play back the recording as you do the exercises, or you may want someone you trust to slowly read the exercises aloud to you as you do them. Alternately, you may want to do the exercises one step at a time, keeping progress notes as you go along. Do the first warm-up exercise, and then choose the method you prefer.

As you progress through the exercises, you'll read more about Graham and how doing these exercises helped him. When you've finished all of the exercises, you'll meet Eliot and Paul, two other men whom OJT has helped in different ways.

Doing these exercises gives you more insight into the effects of your history, and with this insight, you can begin the work of resolving your current personal and relationship struggles. These exercises also opens the storeroom named "My Family History," and it is here that your capacity for personal fulfillment is stored, like covered pieces of furniture in a closed-off, dusty room: your ability to be truthful in one corner, your ability to feel in another, your abilities to understand yourself and communicate each sitting somewhere else, and your playfulness hanging in a closet, covered with cobwebs.

EXERCISE GUIDELINES

Doing this work can make you aware of parts of yourself that you may not have previously recognized, and you might experience emotions that you haven't had before. These reactions are normal and can help with your self-improvement effort, so giving yourself time to process these emotions is important.

Typically in therapy, sessions are fifty minutes long. The guided imagery segment of the session takes about thirty minutes, which is the time allotted for each guided imagery exercise described in this book. In intensive therapy, you would also wait at least one day between sessions to allow your unconscious mind to do the work it needs to do. Similarly, after doing an exercise in this book, you should wait a day before moving on to the next exercise. Doing these exercises will stimulate your unconscious mind, and it's normal for your unconscious mind to continue working after you finish an exercise and complete your progress notes. Pausing for a day will allow the benefits of each exercise to sink in.

During the day that you wait between exercises, it's important that you sit with your feelings from the exercise you just completed. This means that you allow your feelings to surface for approximately five to ten minutes and that you look at the images that your mind's eye shows you, since these images are linked to your feelings. As this is happening, or as soon as possible afterwards, write about how you feel, what you see, and your associations. Since this step is vital to your experiencing a lasting change and feeling more fulfilled, it's restated at the end of each guided imagery exercise in this chapter.

Remember, if you feel anxious at any time, briefly pause, and rest if you need to. Remember too that writing about delays helps to get rid of them.

EXERCISE 1: INTRODUCING GUIDED IMAGERY

Read through the entire exercise before beginning. Then decide if you can remember it, or if you need to record it first and then replay it as you do the exercise, or if you want someone you trust to slowly read it aloud as you do it. As an alternative, do the exercise one step at a time, keeping progress notes as you go along. You'll need about thirty minutes of uninterrupted, quiet time for the entire sequence. You'll be spending one or two minutes between each step to focus in on the images. Remember, you'll be in a daydream, so don't expect what you're doing to make logical sense.

1. Get comfortable, close your eyes, and let your mind's eye look for a small boy. If a boy's image doesn't appear, create one in your mind. He can be an infant, a toddler, or a young teen. If more than one boy appears, focus on the nearest boy. Notice his surroundings. Pay attention to any details that come to you. If you can't see a child, it's okay. Simply imagine he's there, hiding, until he feels safe.

2. Imagine you're able to walk into this imaginary place like you could walk into another room in your home. Picture yourself quietly approaching the boy, imagine he sees you, and you introduce yourself. Again, if you haven't pictured a boy yet, continue, since he is there, somewhere. Realize you're standing in your history, and the boy isn't accustomed to seeing you.

3. Be patient. When you imagine yourself approaching him, he may or may not respond, or look at you. His image may even fade and then return. All of this is normal.

4. Explore the image. What part of your history are you in? Your old home? Some special place where you felt safe? Are others nearby? Who are they? Let the boy know you're interested in his environment.

5. Imagine sitting near him, or imagine just sitting down if he's not yet in view. Realize you're with the boy who's responsible for the caretaking of your early family experiences; he's the ambassador of your history. Notice his age, his facial expression, his clothing, or anything else that catches your mind's eye. If he hides from you, spend this time exploring his environment. Stay in this image as long as you like.

6. When you're ready to leave the image, tell him you enjoyed being there and that you'll return. Imagine telling him you're always there if he needs you, that you're constantly aware of him, and are in his future. As the image fades in your mind's eye, notice how you feel in your body.

7. Write down whatever comes to mind—thoughts, feelings, sensations, and other reactions. Be spontaneous. Don't worry about spelling or punctuation, or if your words make any sense. Simply let your hand "go," as you freely associate.

8. If you haven't already, write down what you imagine this boy needed from his family to feel safe and happy, and what he needs from you to feel this.

WHAT JUST HAPPENED?

Usually, guided imagery is like a deep daydream, in which you forget your immediate surroundings. If someone was reading to you during this exercise, you probably just heard their voice and otherwise forgot about them. Your imagination guided you into the there-and-then, simultaneously working on bridge construction into your boyhood. Your way into this image was illuminated by your mind's eye like the headlights of a car. You sat in the there-and-then, in a part of your history, and met the ambassador for boyhood experiences kept in "My Family History." This is the storehouse, and birthplace, of your capacity for fulfillment. You may feel tired. This is normal when doing emotional OJT work. It's normal, too, not to forget this exercise too quickly.

How old was the boy in your image? You can assume the boy's facial expression indicates how you felt at that age. His age indicates when your feelings began affecting you, and his environment shows you where this began. For example, some men see the boy in their early family home, a happy home with friendly, warm faces everywhere. Others see the boy wandering outside the home, sometimes with his pals, sometimes alone. A few men (like my client Graham) see the boy in an empty, darkened space.

PAUSE

It's time to rest. Please stop here, and continue reading tomorrow, picking up where you left off. During this time between exercises it's important that you sit with your feelings for about five to ten minutes.

This means that you allow your feelings to surface, and you let your mind's eye show you the images that are linked to your feelings. As this happens, or soon afterward, write about your feelings, what you see, and your associations. If you feel anxious, refer to chapter 2 or to the websites in the introduction.

GRAHAM'S ALCOHOL ABUSE

Graham began drinking at age fourteen, and kept on for the next thirty years. At age forty-three, he moved from the East to the West Coast. He fantasized that getting away from his hometown and family would help. This was a classic *geographic*, an effort familiar to many alcoholics, when the drinker tries unsuccessfully to escape his problems. It wasn't long until Graham's binges, drunk driving, and memory blackouts worsened. At times, he'd wake up in his car, in a strange city, panicky, not remembering the night before. Six months after moving, he was arrested for drunk driving.

Walking out of a jail cell, massively ashamed, going to court, were enough. He'd hit bottom. He knew if he continued drinking, he'd probably die, and soon. The part of him in tremendous pain, the young boy, pushed the adult to get help.

Graham attended AA meetings regularly, met with a nutritionist, committed himself to recovery, and along with counseling, he worked steadily at OJT. In progress notes, he wrote about his drinking. Soon he understood that in the aftermath of a binge-drinking episode, his self-disgust re-created how he believed his parents felt about him—disgusted. He recalled feeling more like a roommate than their son. He became detached, learning to blend into the background like a chameleon, and when his parents fought, he imagined he became invisible.

In time, Graham's journeys between *then* and *now* became second nature. He spent time with the boy who felt like a burden in the family. He wrote extensively about his boyhood, and he connected his binges to the pain he felt after meaningless, empty phone conversations with his parents. This work progressed naturally—first tears, anger, then healing, insight, the urge to drink losing its grip, and finally, peace of mind.

Graham began with the same road trips you're taking now. I've taken them too, and like Graham, I continue to take them. Sometimes, as in a tug-of-war, old experiences still pull Graham toward bad choices. But now, he knows these old painful experiences are taxicab and bullet train passengers in need of his care and attention.

EXERCISE 2: JOURNEY TO THE INFANT

It's time to begin your journey. Again, read through this entire exercise before beginning. Decide if you can remember it, or if you need to record it and then play it back as you do the exercise, or if you would rather have someone you trust to slowly read it aloud as you do it. As an alternative, do the exercise one step at a time, keeping progress notes as you go along. You'll need about thirty minutes of uninterrupted, quiet time for the entire exercise. You'll be spending one or two minutes between each step to focus on the images.

1. Get comfortable, close you eyes, slowly take two or three deep breaths, and picture in your mind's eye a young baby boy. As this image forms, notice if this baby is asleep, restless, crying, or quietly lying down. Notice his surroundings.

2. Imagine entering this scene as an adult, gently lift and cradle him in your arms. Picture him resting peacefully, gazing up at you. Neither of you are aware of anything else. Realize you're standing in your own history, holding the tiny ambassador of

all your infant experiences. An enormous job for such a little guy, isn't it?

3. Explore the surroundings in your mind's eye. If you are inside a room, what else is in the room? Is anyone else there? Is the image constant or fading in and out? How are you feeling—calm or anxious or happy or sad?

4. Imagine the sensations you'd feel holding the baby, like the softness and warmth of his skin, the feeling of his face as you gently press it against yours; the baby's clean aroma.

5. Look into the infant's eyes and imagine how he feels being with you. What's he telling you? How is he feeling inside? Imagine seeing your eyes through the baby's eyes. How does your gaze affect him? Is it calming him or making him anxious?

6. Realize your role in this baby's well-being and safety. Know that, as he looks at you, he's looking *into* you, soaking in the care and love he sees in your eyes, and he wants you to know how he feels. In fact, he trusts that you know this, naturally, and that you know what to do for him.

7. Know too, he'll never forget feeling this safe. Being with you is now etched in his mind. He never forgets how it felt to be with you. What more have you given him? Stay in this scene as long as you like.

8. When you're ready, picture placing the baby gently down. Quietly leave the image, and return to the here-and-now. If the baby wasn't visible, leave an imaginary note, telling him you were there and will return. As the image fades, notice how you feel inside.

9. Write your thoughts, feelings, sensations, and other reactions. Be spontaneous. Don't worry about spelling or punctuation, or if your words make any sense. Simply let your hand "go," as you freely associate.

<u>WHAT JUST HAPPENED?</u>

In this second guided imagery exercise, your imagination took you on a journey to the earliest part of your life and continued constructing your bridge. Your mind's eye lit the way, and you sat in your there-and-then with the tiny ambassador of your infant experiences. According to our building code, this little guy didn't feel like a separate person: instead he felt that others were an extension of him, there to do his bidding. You can assume the infant's facial expression and level of relaxation indicates how you felt then, and his surroundings suggest a time when you began storing experiences in your there-and-then.

Consider the similarities between a new baby and a new relationship. When you consider what an infant needs, it's similar to the needs of a "newborn" relationship. Think about what your needs are in a new relationship. Do they include being loved? Being in control? Being worshipped? Expecting your partner to obey you? Scaring your partner?

How you imagined the infant felt in his tiny body (if he was calm or anxious or happy or sad) is probably similar to your reactions in a new relationship. When you looked through the infant's eyes into your own, you saw what a new partner is likely to see. You'll read more about this in a later chapter of this book.

<u>PAUSE</u>

It's time to rest. Please stop here, and continue reading tomorrow, picking up where you left off. During this time between exercises it's important that you sit with your feelings for about five to ten minutes. This means that you allow your feelings to surface, and you let your mind's eye show you the images that are linked to your feelings. As this happens, or soon afterward, write about your feelings, what you see, and your associations. If you feel anxious, refer to chapter 2 or to the websites in the introduction.

GRAHAM'S ROAD TRIP TO THE INFANT

When Graham first tried to take a journey to the infant, he confronted his struggle with attachments. He described how, for him, a baby's cries were like fingernails on a chalkboard. No matter where he was, when a baby cried, he had to get away. If he couldn't get away, he'd get angry. And if he could get away, he'd drink. His reactions all had a single goal—to distract him from the cries.

The techniques covered in chapter 2 helped Graham overcome his resistance. First he had to learn to separate from the infant's cries. Then he could see his reaction for what it was, running away from the screaming infant inside himself. After doing guided imagery exercises and keeping progress notes every day for a week, he could visit the baby, comfort him, and tell him about parents who were incapable of care.

At about week six, his urge to drink began to fade, and a baby's cries no longer disturbed him. Even though he had clear evidence of progress, however, he continued at times to distrust his own reactions. He'd read earlier progress notes to remind himself that he was feeling better.

Graham carries a photograph of the infant, taken when he was two weeks old, and sometimes he'll talk to the infant in the picture. (This is a conventional technique in self-improvement work and can help you reconnect with parts of yourself.) He'll look into the baby's eyes and imagine how the little guy felt in the arms of his drunken mother. He imagines the stench of her alcohol breath hitting him in the face like a slap. Then, any urge he feels to run, or to drink, stops.

EXERCISE 3: JOURNEY TO THE TODDLER

It's time for the next stage of your journey. Again, read through this entire exercise before beginning and choose the method you prefer for doing the exercise. (See methods described in exercises 1 and 2.) Set aside about thirty minutes of uninterrupted quiet time for the entire exercise, allowing about one to two minutes of quiet between each step to focus in on the images.

1. Get comfortable, close your eyes, slowly breathing in and out two or three times, and picture a small boy about age two or three, quietly sitting among his toys, playing.

2. Explore the image. Is the environment familiar? Are you home again? How does this little guy feel? What toys do you see? Are your parents there? Is the boy safe?

3. Visualize him approaching you, curiously touching your face, your shirt, looking into your eyes, then running back to his toys, squealing with laughter. Listen and watch as he makes noises and gestures, trying to communicate with you. What's he trying to tell you?

4. Picture playing together. Realize these moments with you are now part of his there-and-then, especially his sense of connection to you, him feeling safe, being loved, and having you as a playmate. Know that these moments with you will remain with him forever.

5. When you're ready to leave the image, let the little guy know. Tell him you had fun, and you'll play with him soon, and you'll bring him a new toy, something from the future. Picture walking away, looking back, seeing him playing alone, deep in fantasies. Return to the here-and-now, and notice how you feel.

6. Write down whatever comes to mind. Be spontaneous; don't worry about what or how you're writing, or if your words make any sense. Simply let your hand "go," expressing anything that comes to mind.

7. If you haven't already done so, write what you imagine a toddler needs from you to feel safe, loved, and happy. Rest if you need to.

WHAT JUST HAPPENED?

Your imagination took you on a road trip to a time when, according to our building code, life was mostly experienced as all good or all bad. Your mind's eye helped you find your way to the playful part of you, which is still important in your life. This topic will be covered more in later chapters.

Based on the boy's expressions, you saw how the small boy typically felt at this age. You noticed the toddler's age, which, according to our building code, is about the time you began storing "good or bad" experiences. You may know people who view life in black and white, good or bad terms. It helps to think of them as being stuck at the toddler's age in terms of how they form attachments and relate. As their partner, you're either wonderful or detested.

Remember, doing these exercises strengthens the connection between your conscious mind and your unconscious mind. This is the work of OJT, building and reinforcing your bridge while you travel on it.

PAUSE

It's time to rest. Please stop here, and continue reading tomorrow, picking up where you left off. During this time between exercises it's important that you sit with your feelings for about five to ten minutes. This means that you allow your feelings to surface, and you let your mind's eye show you the images that are linked to your feelings. As this happens, or soon afterward, write about your feelings, what you see, and your associations. If you feel anxious, refer to chapter 2 or to the websites in the introduction.

GRAHAM'S ROAD TRIP TO THE TODDLER AND LOSING THE URGE TO DRINK

Road trips to the toddler helped Graham understand his binge drinking. Here's how it happened.

For several weeks, Graham had been using guided imagery and free association consistently outside of therapy. He regularly attended AA meetings and was keeping up with his progress notes. Even though his drinking urges had faded, he became frustrated whenever they did reoccur. He wanted them to stop completely. He called me to schedule an appointment, but I reminded Graham he had everything he needed to deal with this struggle.

I told him he'd forgotten about the part of himself that will always think and feel alcoholically, and that this is what alcoholics often do early on in recovery. He'd forgotten that there's a permanent part of him that searches for reasons to take "just one" drink, or do anything to sabotage his sobriety. I suggested he do more guided imagery and revisit the toddler. I knew that this was the period of his life when his parents divorced and he was sent away from home. It was the point in his life when his attachments to his family collapsed. The pain he felt over this loss was what he had learned to submerge by drinking, typically when he felt the slightest rejection from other people. He needed to learn how to deal with the pain. I suggested that whatever he saw in the images of himself as a toddler would help him understand his urges to drink and why these urges will never completely disappear. Two weeks passed before Graham called again, and then we met to talk about the work he'd done on his own.

When Graham arrived with his progress notes, his face and voice conveyed confidence. He read aloud from the notes about his most recent guided imagery work. He had imagined himself riding on a magic carpet into his own history. He could see the toddler standing on his aunt's porch, silently peering out over the top of his suitcase, watching his parents' car drive off. In this scene, the boy's face looked like stone.

Graham saw himself landing the carpet next to the child, lifting up the boy onto the carpet, and the two of them flying away. He read of the boy's fear that the carpet would crash, and how he had reassured the boy they were both safe. He invited the boy to be his copilot as they flew the carpet together and talked to the boy about what had happened in his family. He told the boy he was sorry it had taken thirty years to rescue him but that now his pain would stop.

He read about how, as he put his arm around the boy, he could feel the texture of the boy's shirt. Graham imagined the boy sleeping peacefully on the carpet as they sailed back into the here-and-now. Graham described their landing—the little boy still asleep—and then he too fell asleep for several minutes in my office chair. When he awoke, he'd changed. He was playful, laughing and wishing he'd awakened to find the boy with him. He talked about the boy always being with him, along with the remnants of his history that will remain sources of pain, his random urges to drink, and the magic carpet's availability.

The next morning Graham called me, excited about a dream he'd had the night before. In this dream, the boy raged at the family for all the destruction; he kicked, screamed, and cried the way the boy never did or could. Graham described how, after having this dream, he "couldn't find" his rage inside himself. A few weeks later, other life changes had gained traction. He said he no longer felt like a burden and no longer felt troubled by infant cries. Urges to drink rarely happen now, and when they do, he remembers the magic carpet.

EXERCISE 4: JOURNEY TO THE TEENAGER

Again, read through this entire exercise before beginning and choose the method you prefer for doing the exercise. (See methods described in exercises 1 and 2). Set aside about thirty minutes of uninterrupted quiet time for the entire exercise, allowing about one to two minutes of quiet between each step to focus in on the images.

1. Get comfortable, close your eyes, slowly breathing in and out two or three times, and then picture a young teenage boy, about age thirteen, sitting somewhere quiet, as though he's waiting for you.

2. Imagine entering this scene as an adult and sitting near him. Realize you're in your own history and that this boy is the ambassador of your history up to this time in your life. He carries all your life experiences, the good, the bad, and the ugly. A big responsibility for a young boy, isn't it? Notice how you feel sitting there.

3. Explore this image. Is the environment familiar? Are others in the image? How are you feeling inside?

4. Look at the boy. Let him know you're glad to see him. Notice his mood, his appearance, grooming, and facial expressions. Tell him you're from his future. Tell him that he's the ambassador of all your boyhood experiences up to this point in time.

5. Realize that this boy could use some words of kindness; something teenage boys need a lot of. What was it like in your family at this age? Did you hear kind words at home?

6. Imagine talking with him, asking about his interests, hobbies, and goals. Listen to whatever he says, knowing that he's eager

to talk about his life and that he may feel awkward, like most teens talking to grownups. Tell him to take all the time he needs, that whatever he says is worth listening to. Tell him too that sometimes people communicate without words and imagine he believes you.

7. Recognize he's soaking up this experience like a sponge. It will be a part of his history, and he'll use it as a guide on his road trip to being a man. He'll take this connected feeling, the sense that he matters, that whatever he says to you is worth saying, and that you're there because you simply wanted to be.

8. When you're ready to leave this image, let him know it's time for you to go, that you're happy you met and that you'll return. Picture walking away, looking back, seeing him quietly relax. Return to the here-and-now, and notice how you feel.

9. Write down whatever comes to mind. Be spontaneous; don't worry about what or how you're writing, or if your words make any sense. Simply let your hand "go," and expressing anything that comes to mind.

10. If you haven't already done so, write down what a young teen needs from you to feel safe, content, and loved. Write about how you wanted to matter enough in your family to have your thoughts and feelings recognized. Rest if you need to.

WHAT JUST HAPPENED?

Your imagination took you to the young teen, the ambassador of most of your boyhood experiences. You saw how you felt at this age. Boys at this age are often anxious about being older but usually conceal it. They have sexual urges. They feel physically strong, sometimes invincible, yet underneath this, they're often frightened by what lies ahead. In your image of the teen, you acknowledged his place in life, and let him know you value his world—an experience that older boys desperately need from men who care about them. It's what you needed as well, and if this recognition was absent, you might now begin to feel the sadness and anger that you've "put behind you" since you were a boy.

PAUSE

It's time to rest. Please stop here, and continue reading tomorrow, picking up where you left off. During this time between exercises it's important that you sit with your feelings for about five to ten minutes. This means that you allow your feelings to surface, and you let your mind's eye show you the images that are linked to your feelings. As this happens, or soon afterward, write about your feelings, what you see, and your associations. If you feel anxious, refer to chapter 2 or to the websites in the introduction.

GRAHAM'S ROAD TRIP TO THE TEEN

During his road trip to the teen, Graham recalled playing high school football and how this helped him vent frustration and anger. He remembered his coaches talking to him about managing his anger on and off the playing field. Still, he remembers using aggression to keep others away, even though he ached for friendships, and taking his first drink at age thirteen.

While he was an average ball player, he excelled academically. He loved reading history; it helped him imagine the lives and worlds of others. He also found solace in the abstract world of science and math. He easily avoided his family, using "studying" as an excuse. As his grades improved, the admiration and encouragement he received from teachers gave him a sense of value. Still, he kept drinking and aching for connection.

He recalled the first time he came home drunk at age fourteen and his father threatened to slice off both of Graham's hands if he drank again. But there was no turning back. He drank alcoholically from the first drink to the last, thirty years later. He wrote extensively about the loss of his relationship with his father and how his binge drinking was connected with this loss. He recalled times that he'd left work, sometimes midday, to drink away feelings of rejection that he had imagined were coming from interactions with his male colleagues. Now he realized that these feelings were, on a deeper level, associated with his father's rejection of him as a child. The original pain of his father's rejection would swell up inside him and to numb this pain, he had to drink.

EXERCISE 5: JOURNEY TO YOUR PARENTS

It's time to visit your parents as children. Again, read through this entire exercise before beginning and choose the method you prefer for doing the exercise. (See methods described in exercises 1 and 2). Set aside about thirty minutes of uninterrupted quiet time for the entire exercise, allowing about one to two minutes of quiet between each step to focus in on the images.

Note that in this exercise, you may choose to visit each parent separately. You may also visit other important people from your boyhood, such as a teacher, an aunt, an uncle, or a sibling. A few men choose to visit people who traumatized them when they were boys. You can modify the following steps to imagine the person you wish to visit in your history.

1. Get comfortable, close your eyes, slowly breathing in and out two or three times. Picture each of your parents as an adult, and then imagine them slowly becoming younger until you see them as children, approximately seven to ten years old.

If you were raised by a single parent, simply rely on your imagination to provide an image of your other parent.

2. Imagine entering this scene as the adult you are today, letting them know who you are, that you're from their future, and that they will grow to become your parents. Realize that you are standing in your parents' histories, that you absorbed their histories like a sponge throughout your boyhood, and that you carry this with you. As you do this, notice how you're feeling in your body.

3. Say to them that, like all children, they too need love and care, but that you know from your own history that this didn't happen to them as often as it should have.

4. Notice their mood, their facial expressions, and their appearance. Get at eye level with both of them, and look *into* them. How are these two small children feeling? Are they happy to see you? Afraid? Pleading for love? Wanting to be alone?

5. Tell them they're always with you and that you're with them. Imagine holding each of them, extending your care and love, telling them you'll be back soon.

6. Now walk away from the image and return into the here-and-now. Take as much time as you need, allowing these images to fade away.

7. Write down whatever comes to mind. Be spontaneous; don't worry about what or how you're writing, or if your words make any sense. Simply let your hand "go," expressing anything that comes to mind.

8. If you haven't already done so, write down what a young child needs from you to feel safe, content, and that he matters. Write about how you wanted to matter enough in your family

to have your thoughts and feelings recognized. Rest if you need to.

WHAT JUST HAPPENED?

Throughout your boyhood, the experience of being with your parents was permanently imprinted in your unconscious mind's "My Family History." Very early in life, you naturally concluded that this is how *all* relationships should feel, and you've maintained this perspective your entire life. You had little choice. Even if you don't remember early family experiences, early impressions are etched in your mind. They are a "living record" (Hedges, 1994), replaying old family themes 24/7 as background music in the movie of your life.

Seeing your parents as children helps you stop blaming them for what they couldn't provide. And it helps you stop blaming those who care about you today for not knowing what, when, or how you want something. You realize your parents did all they could do, which is to give you what their parents gave them. Despite their inadequacies or frailties as parents, they were once lovable children, wanting the same things you want.

PAUSE

It's time to rest. Please stop here, and continue reading tomorrow, picking up where you left off. During this time between exercises it's important that you sit with your feelings for about five to ten minutes. This means that you allow your feelings to surface, and you let your mind's eye show you the images that are linked to your feelings. As this happens, or soon afterward, write about your feelings, what you see, and your associations. If you feel anxious, refer to chapter 2 or to the websites in the introduction.

GRAHAM'S ROAD TRIP TO HIS PARENTS

After several months of self-improvement work and sporadic counseling, Graham felt himself again descending into a dark place inside him. When he called, I encouraged him to focus his imagery work and progress notes on spending some time with his parents as children. I suggested again that finding empathy for his parents was essential to his healing.

For some time, Graham had resisted doing this particular exercise. He had great difficulty picturing himself as an adult with his parents as children. To resolve this difficulty, he imagined himself to be a child of the same age as them. As he did this, he could picture being with them. Whereas the adult Graham had struggled with forgiving his parents, the boy was willing to forgive the children who would one day send him away. He easily imagined playing with these two children, and in this way, he began to accept that his parents had done all they could for him throughout their lives as grownups. For several weeks after doing this exercise, Graham pictured these three children playing quietly together, and he wrote extensively about how each of them felt.

Reviewing what happened in this exercise helps Graham stay mindful of the there-and-then needs that he sometimes projects into his adult interactions, such as giving others responsibility for his feelings. His progress notes now show him doing this less often.

EXERCISE 6: BRIDGE REINFORCEMENT

You'll need about thirty minutes in a quiet, stationary place, away from everyday distractions. No preparation is needed. You'll simple read, imagine, feel, think, and write.

This exercise illustrates how boyhood patterns can impact your life today. Like other exercises, it reinforces your bridge's capacity so feelings and reactions that need your attention can move across. If you do not see the images, don't worry. Your unconscious mind keeps some experiences in the there-and-then until you're able to manage them, and remember, you can always come back to any exercise. Your progress notes will help you understand which early relationship you're still struggling with.

First, picture a time you felt unimportant to your parent(s). Naturally you'd feel like you were in an emotional tug-of-war—wanting to approach your parent(s) but fearing consequences. You might try different strategies, like acting silly or acting like an adult or entertaining or having tantrums or faking an illness. If this was true, when you feel unimportant as an adult, you'd have similar struggles, and you might try these old approaches. Without self-improvement you'd be unaware of the strong influence your early experiences would have.

Let's look at how this might show up today. You're at work, and need to speak to your coworker. It's urgent. You see he's in another discussion, you start to approach, and out of the blue, a wave of fear washes over you. You picture his angry response, even though he's never been angry before. So you stop, walk away, and pace the floor until your coworker has finished his conversation. When you give him the urgent message, he does get angry with you—for not interrupting him before!

At this point in reading this book, it's probably clear to you that your out-of-the-blue fear would have been your association to an early experience of feeling like you intruded. You'd know that the bullet train arrived, the boy unpacked his suitcase of fear, and you react today like you reacted then—you withdraw in fear.

Let's look at another example. Despite your fear, you interrupt your coworker's conversation with an old attention-getting strategy.

For instance, you become an entertainer, and interrupt him with a dumb remark or a bad joke. The result is the same: no matter what you do, you feel like a nuisance, and your coworker is angered by your foolishness.

Picture and write about your parents' relationship when you were a boy. The time period that comes to mind is the one you'll need.

When parents argue without end, or when boys seldom observe parents happy, they can grow up anxious or afraid. If this happened to you, you're vulnerable to having these same reactions at the sound of any argument. Let's say you're watching a film, and there's a scene involving conflict, and out of the blue, you feel panicky and leave the room. Boyhood emotions remain powerful—until you start visiting the boy.

Alternatively, if your parents usually reconnected after fighting, and you saw or heard this happen, conflict today might not be full of emotional twists and turns. Instead, you'd develop a relational pattern of love-conflict-resolution, and as an adult you'd be confident that arguments can end without resentment. You would trust your partner during a fight. You would know that the relationship is intact, even while you fight.

Stop here and write progress notes about recent contacts with someone close to you or people at work or people in your community. In what ways are these events similar to your experiences as a boy?

CASE STUDIES

The stories that follow show how two men with very different problems both benefited from OJT. These stories are not detailed descriptions but, rather, are quick sketches to convey important points. Because of their initial circumstances, both men began self-improvement in counseling, but self-improvement is something you can do on your own.

ELIOT

Eliot, age forty-seven, a branch manager at a large office supply store, married, father to two boys, ages five and seven years, began counseling and self-improvement to stop fights with his wife. In the past month, fights were more frequent and left unresolved. The last fight, one week earlier, scared him and his family—he'd punched a hole in the living room wall. Since then, he and his wife hadn't talked, except about the boys. The youngest was wetting his bed, and their playtimes were more aggressive.

Eliot recounted fights with his wife. "She's been complaining a lot that I don't hear her. When I repeat back what she says, word for word, she gets angrier, telling me 'You're just proving my point—you're not listening!' and walks away. She tells me I don't care about her feelings. This last time, when I asked for specifics, she told me 'After nine years together, you should know what's bothering me!' Then she walked away." He remembered how helpless he felt just before punching the wall. "Seeing her walk away threw me over the edge." Now he was scared. He wasn't normally violent, and he'd injured himself.

My remark "Women seem to swim in a pool of emotions, 24/7" didn't affect him. His blank expression showed confusion, which was probably what his wife saw, and told me he knew little about her, or his own, emotions. When I asked how he felt about my remark, he said it irritated him, like his wife's remark. We talked about his general reaction to not knowing. It both irritated and scared him. His fear was about feeling ashamed, and his irritation was toward himself.

Most men don't enjoy fear, anger, or shame. Eliot was eager to try guided imagery, less so with free association until he wrote a few thoughts down and read them later. Looking down at his bandaged hand, he imagined a boy about age eight. Instead of approaching the boy in the image, he began freely associating. (This is normal. Sometimes there's a need to get reacquainted with the there-and-then before stepping into it.)

"I remember being a kid, and my parents' fights. I never knew what to do. I'd see my mother's blank face. She got that look whenever they fought. She'd try arguing with Dad, but once she had that look, she'd leave the room. After that, they wouldn't talk for days. I knew not to say much. She had that look for days, and Dad would just retreat into the garage." After these associations, he could imagine the boy. Telling me about the image helped lower his anxiety during the initial road trip.

In the image, the boy sat quietly in his room, scared. I encouraged Eliot to simply sit with the boy, letting the boy know he mattered. After several minutes of silence, Eliot returned to the here-and-now, but taxicabs kept arriving in the counseling room, and the suitcases started opening.

Still looking at his hand, he associated to age twelve, getting hurt playing ball, and how this annoyed his mother. He talked about being sick, how she'd put medicine on his nightstand, and stand in the doorway to check in on him, saying "I don't want you to make me sick." When his father yelled at her about this, Eliot felt all the more like a burden.

The lack of care in boyhood, and his confusion and anger about it, had become lodged in Eliot's "My Family History." The anger, confusion, and struggle to connect with his wife connected him to history, stirring up emotional ghosts. I spoke about the normal travel of taxicabs, the bullet train, suitcases, how they'd continue arriving, and how this builds a bridge between then and now. We talked about the last fight, the hole in the wall, the boy's rage that boarded the bullet train, and how the train kept going, right through the living room wall. He started keeping progress notes after the first session.

In our second session, Eliot learned that, according to our building code, dreaming is his unconscious mind working on unresolved and sometimes deeply troubling emotions. One particular dream was symbolic: his first bicycle, rolling slowly down the sidewalk, without a passenger. He took a road trip to the boy and saw himself sitting alone, scared and lonely. Later, he realized he felt the same way when he fought with his wife.

Now, Eliot's there-and-then regularly unpacks in the here-and-now, as he imagines sitting with his arm around the boy, or holding the infant, or being with the teen, and giving each young ambassador his love and care. He and his wife talk openly about their early experiences, and each realizes how little they knew about the other's history. They learned through these conversations what it was that brought them together: like two peas in a pod; their early experiences were quite similar. Their connection deepened, as it often does, when partners learn more about each other's pain. Now, she invites him to talk or read her his progress notes whenever he feels safe enough to do so.

PAUL

Paul, age forty-one, was referred by his employee assistance program. For the past three years he'd worked as a physician's assistant at a children's hospital and recently was cited for his aggressive behavior. Coworkers complained of his aggressive attitude, claimed he was unfriendly toward some patients, particularly those children who cried during treatment. When one patient's parent overheard his remarks about her son, she complained. He was placed on probationary status and asked to enter therapy. His job, and career, were in jeopardy.

Married for five years, father of twins, a boy and girl age nine, Paul described his current home life as "mostly okay." This, plus his vague descriptions of his family of origin, hinted at troubled early attachments. In our first few sessions, we also talked about the seriousness of his situation. I noticed my irritation at his minimizing his employer's concerns. Because of our building code, I knew this might be how his parents felt about him. Was he replaying an old family theme of people being angry with him? Was he acting out his boyhood anger with verbal aggression toward coworkers and toward children?

I told him of my irritation and about my associations to his parents. I expected more aggression, and instead, he softened. He saw my surprise and remarked "Not many people really know how I feel." Since he worked with children, I assumed the boy was accessible and asked him to close his eyes and look inside. He saw the boy, about age twelve, and spoke with him about the boy's dream of being a firefighter. He heard his father's voice, opposing the boy's dream, and the boy faded from the image. He recalled his father saying "Both you and your brother will be doctors, like I am, and like your grandfather was. Forget anything else!"

Bridge building began quickly. I educated Paul to the unconscious mind and how I imagined that he had a crawl-rope bridge that allowed his history, his rage, to move into the present. Given the limited capacity of his bridge, it didn't surprise me that his nearest target was the children needing his care.

He repeated the first four road trips many times, both with me and at home. Suitcases full of rage started showing up. The fifth journey was hard, and several weeks passed before he could spend time with his parents, and he could only do this in the counseling room. This isn't uncommon. Bringing empathy to parents responsible for our pain isn't always easy.

Paul kept progress notes between counseling appointments. His homework included progress notes about each child he met that day. He wrote about what he imagined the child needed, from the child's parents and from him. After three months of hard work, he made the connection between his history and the crying children. He understood why taxicabs and an occasional bullet train would arrive at his work. Looking at children in pain and mocking them was his bleak attempt at stopping his own pain.

Counseling shifted to his grief and loss about having no relationship with his father. Paul freely associated about the longstanding family tension and his father's absence for most of Paul's first five years of life. He recalled the disastrous impact of his father's diabetes and his partial blindness at age forty-two.

The hopes and dreams of the family faded with his father's vision. Paul felt guilty, since his father often blamed his illness on having to work so hard for the family. "The least you could do is follow in my footsteps!" he'd say. His father's rage and his guilt about having independent dreams were both imprinted in his there-and-then.

With continued road trips across the ever-widening bridge, Paul's guilt subsided and he could grieve the loss of a father-son connection. Exercise 5 helped him realize that his demanding supervisor felt like being with his father. At this point, he recognizes what the children need from him. We've talked about alternatives, and he's now a volunteer fireman, teaching children at local schools about fire prevention and giving kids at his work little firemen hats.

THE ROAD AHEAD

Chapter 5 introduces the tools you will use to apply what you've learned so far. As you will see, what you've learned about yourself can be helpful in many areas of your life.

Chapter 5
The Open Road

Having a free-flowing connection between *then* and *now* provides you with numerous opportunities for changing your life for the better. This is a result of the bridge-building work you've already done.

You have developed a skill set to help identify when, where, and why you reenact your history. You can now identify when you want to change this, to stop reenacting your history and do something different. The next step is to look at how you can use bridge building in your relationships. The goal of this chapter is to help you respond differently to difficult emotional situations, so that the roadway connecting you and your partner remains open. And if you're not in a relationship at this time, this chapter will help you prepare for a relationship in your future.

Before continuing, please stop to look at the work you've done so far. It's a huge accomplishment, and this is a good time to gauge this for yourself. Set aside some time to read through your progress notes, comparing your earliest to your most recent entries.

TAKING THE NEXT STEP

Advancing through OJT can be compared to climbing the ladder of success professionally. Both require facing new challenges. Having more insight and greater self-understanding brings you closer to happiness, and you now have a new challenge—putting these skills into practice.

If you think "I already know how to make changes," you're right. You'd probably start the way most men do—using patterns you learned long ago. Generally, along with boyhood experiences, boyhood approaches to change arrive in the here-and-now, usually in the next taxicab. While an old approach to change might work, you need to be able to recognize when it won't and apply a different approach that will. Similarly, if you were promoted at your job, skills you had developed for an earlier task might no longer be useful and you would need to acquire some new skills.

This chapter reviews four *mindsets*, or fundamental approaches, you may use in emotional situations: fixing; repairing; prevention, and preparation. It also discusses the possible outcomes of these approaches, or what often happens when you apply these mindsets in everyday life when issues arise. For example, sometimes a quick fix works; but more often than not, taking this approach can be disastrous. The exercises in this chapter will help you understand how to approach change and how you can alter your approach to improve your life and relationships. (For editorial purposes only, in the following sections your partner's gender is assumed to be female.)

FIXING

For our purposes, *fixing* means taking quick action, not to resolve a situation, but to do whatever it takes to block a feeling. Often, men unknowingly react to emotional situations with one goal: "How fast can I stop what I'm feeling?" While not bad or wrong, this mindset often leads to disaster; you end up exhausted, simply because you've jumped to conclusions. For instance, your partner tells you about her struggle with the kids, and instead of hearing her ask for your empathy, you tell her what she should do. You do this because you're uncomfortable feeling empathic. Then, when she gets angry, you're confused. Fixing a situation may give you temporary relief, but it seldom lasts, and fixing often makes situations worse. When the situation does get worse, many of us get confused, thinking "I fixed it, didn't I?"

This mindset often shows up in our relationships. Generally, women enjoy talking more than men, especially in close relationships. While it may seem your partner talks into the air, this usually relaxes her, and sometimes she's freely associating. This is normal. Our tendency to be fixers may come up when we feel challenged by what our partner is saying. This can happen in an argument or even in a tender moment, if it stirs up old hurts.

Many of us make the mistake of thinking that we have to react quickly to stop a bad feeling from getting worse. As we listen to the words, we interpret what our partner says. Sometimes we're right, but many times we interpret our partner's remarks as criticism. Then our fear of inadequacy or our confusion or our irritation surges, and we react, wanting to stop our feeling fast, like an emergency room physician clamping off an artery.

At work and outside our relationship, we usually can benefit from thinking logically. This is comfortable, and we try using this approach at home. The problem is most women don't think logically in these situations. Instead, they feel their way through emotional issues and while they know we prefer logic, emotions have no logic. This is one reason that many of us hear "You're not listening to me, again!" after our well-intended fast action to end an argument.

Your challenge is to realize that when your partner talks, what you're hearing may not be a call to action. Try this response instead: "If something's wrong, I have no idea what it is. But I'm right here, listening. Just let me know if you need my help." I can almost guarantee that you'll have a better relationship. Ask your partner, or women you know, about this.

WHY WE FIX

Fixing is what we do in difficult situations to stop our discomfort. Since discomfort often results from our misinterpretations, fixing means that we don't give ourselves the opportunity to find out what the other person actually meant. Even with bridge building well underway or completed, certain emotional situations will cause us to act fast, especially if what we feel is what we felt as a boy. Here's an example.

Imagine an argument with your partner. You're feeling stuck, trapped. While this feeling is vaguely familiar, right now, you just want out of the argument. You're tired and not interested in where or when you felt this way before. You wait for the right moment, and then say, "We're going nowhere, fast. You're right. I'll do whatever you want, but let's just stop." Your partner agrees. You've fixed the situation, but you had to give in. You walk away, irritated.

Let's assume you've had this feeling of being trapped since you were a boy, but you've never thought about it. According to our building code, the way you avoided feeling trapped in the argument with your partner—by surrendering—is similar to what you did as a boy. Your irritation today is the boy's irritation, and you remember feeling stuck, listening to your mother's never-ending lectures.

During your argument with your partner, the taxicab carrying the boy's feeling arrives, the suitcase opens, and you feel like you felt then. Then, the next taxicab carrying your boyhood approach arrives, and you do what you did as a kid when you lied your way out of your mother's lectures. Like the boy did, you fabricate excuses for why the argument needs to stop. You may even use the boy's words.

EXERCISE 7: FIXING

This exercise takes about fifteen minutes, including making progress notes. Choose a comfortable environment, such as the one you used in earlier exercises.

1. Remember a time when you fixed a situation. Whatever situation that comes to mind will do. Examples include how you quickly ended an argument you couldn't win, how you covered up an embarrassing mistake at work, what you did when you were caught cheating, a time you gave a gift to ease your guilt, or any other time you felt like you patched up a situation.

2. To help identify the feeling you avoided, notice your associations and how you're feeling now.

3. Write a brief description of the situation, including all you remember about how you and others felt, what you did, and what happened.

4. Are you satisfied, now, with what you did then to fix the situation? Write about this.

5. How long did the fix last? Has the problem troubled you since? Write about this.

PROJECTION – AN UNCONSCIOUS ATTEMPT AT FIXING

Fixing often happens unconsciously, as you attempt to help ward off here-and-now emotional pain. Your unconscious mind, like everyone else's, stores a variety of defense mechanisms. Imagine your unconscious mind can make selections from a menu of defenses, depending on your current situation and your emotional development.

These defenses arrive by taxicab or aboard bullet trains to fix the situation by fighting off the painful feeling in the here-and-now. One defense that commonly arrives is known as "projection." This is when you give your struggle to your partner.

Say you've struggled with your weight. After several months, you're still heavy, and your self-esteem sinks to a new low. You're irritated and want relief. One night before going out to dinner, when your self-esteem is especially low and your trousers especially tight, you say to your partner, "Honey, that's a great dress...a little tight on you, but still, a great color." When she locks herself in the bedroom, crying, you say you're confused, but almost instantly, you're relieved. Now, she feels fat, and you can concentrate on doing some good—calming her down—and you feel better. You've given her your feeling of being fat and your irritation. And if this isn't enough relief, you'll continue projecting, blaming her for ruining the evening and being too sensitive.

WHY WE PROJECT

Why does projecting seem to help in this situation? After all, you'd still be overweight.

Say that, lately, each time you weigh yourself or see your reflection or overhear comments about your weight, your false self-image cracks, like an ice pond with too many skaters. Exploring your history, you'd realize that you've fantasized about people admiring you and how this fantasy holds back the pain of feeling unloved. Now, the more you weigh, the more your self-image, along with your self-confidence, cracks, slowly destroying the imaginary mirror that, up to now, served you so well. Now, your projections are like imaginary strips of tape, holding together this imaginary mirror and your sense of self.

Being a "doormat" is another form that projection can take. As a doormat, you'll do anything to avoid conflict, fantasizing other people will care because you do this. In your mind, you're protecting them. But avoiding arguments is your camouflage; it allows you to reenact being "a good little boy," which got you noticed when you were young. Since your parents usually ignored you, you did whatever you could to please them.

Sometimes, doormats succeed at stopping disagreements. But at a deeper level, as a doormat, you are fending off the pain that comes from not mattering to your parents or from feeling like a failure because your obedience didn't stop your parents' fights. Now, each time you intervene or let people walk all over you, you imagine you're a good little boy. Unless you act like a doormat, you feel useless.

Sadly, when you're a doormat, people eventually get angry with you, like your parents did, and avoid you. This anger stems from your actions as a doormat. For instance, when you and your partner begin fighting, you may try harder to please her so that she stops being angry with you. But when you try to stop the fight, instead of her feeling heard and understood and free to express herself, your partner feels shut out, resentful, and helpless.

Your defenses will persist until your bridge can accommodate the flow of there-and-then pain into the present, so it can heal. Like driving your car on a temporary spare tire, fixing, in all its forms, is a remedy and seldom the solution. Like concrete barriers spanning your bridge, fixing can also be hazardous, even destructive, personally and professionally. If you're not sure if you're a fixer, ask yourself again.

Stop here and think about your approach to change. Do you use projection, act like a doormat, or in some other way try to fix an emotionally difficult situation? Do you make plans to stop a fight that you imagine will happen? What happened to your initiative? Can you see the price you're paying, in terms of your aliveness? Write down your experiences in your progress notes. Later, when you reread them, you'll realize how your thinking is improving. For example, you'll read about what worried you when you began OJT and compare that way of thinking to how you think about the same issue now.

REPAIRING

For our purposes, when you *repair,* you focus on understanding an uncomfortable feeling rather than avoiding it. You still want to stop the feeling, but rather than find a way to leave, you talk about it. If you don't have this book's OJT skills, you'd admit you don't know where to begin. Still, you're willing to work hard to find your way through, not around, an uncomfortable emotional situation.

Take the earlier "fixing" example, and see how "repairing" would help. Recapping, you feel stuck and trapped in an argument with your partner and you just want out, so you surrender. You've found a fast way out of your discomfort, your partner agreed to this, but instead of being happy, you become irritated. Picking up from the point when you began to feel bad and wanted to stop the argument, repairing begins with you saying something like the following: "Let's stop here, okay? We're not getting anywhere. I don't know why, but right now, I feel like running. I have no idea where this comes from, but I don't want to run."

Alternately, depending on your OJT progress, you might also say the following: "Let me think about this, and we'll talk again later. I just don't want us to keep getting stuck like this, and maybe my running is what keeps us stuck. It sure feels familiar." Or you might say, "Right now, I want to run away from you. I have no idea why, but it's not going to help us if I do. Let's find someone we can talk to."

To begin repairing the situation, you would start with asking yourself, "When have I felt this way before?" This question accesses "My Family History" in your unconscious mind, and, if you have felt this way before, this earlier experience takes a taxi to the here-and-now. For instance, in our example of fixing, you'd recognize that today's emotional situation reminds you of how you felt as a teen, listening to the umpteenth lecture from your mother about your friends, homework, and being lazy. You hated these lectures, and you looked for a way out. But wanting to be with mom and, at the same time, wanting to get away was a painful tug of war, and this situation would leave you irritated.

Soon, like a little army general, as a boy you learned to strategize when you were in this situation. You'd think to yourself, "Maybe she'll run out of breath, or maybe I can make her laugh, or maybe I'll say I need to use the bathroom." Over time, you became adept at finding a way out of feeling stuck with her. This strategy eventually became a living record that replays whenever you feel stuck.

Repairing would include telling your partner about this image. You'd talk about the boy's strategies working, how you've relied on them, and how you want to stop. And you would recognize that as a boy, you did all you could, but like most kids, you couldn't communicate feelings or help your family's bad situations. Still, you did all you could to feel valued.

EXERCISE 8: REPAIRING

1. Remember a time you tried to "fix" an emotional situation in your relationship, or ask your partner to remind you of one of these times.

2. Try to picture this scene. This imagery usually brings back the feeling that you tried to squash by using the "fixing" approach.

3. Think about why you needed to sit on the feeling and what you can do differently now to repair the situation. For example, can you tell your partner the truth about what happened and why? Or can you write about it and admit the truth to yourself about the feeling you didn't want to feel?

PREVENTION

Most of us know someone who exudes self-confidence. This is the guy who knows he'll find his way through just about anything, if it happens. This guy thinks, "I haven't the slightest idea what I'll do, but when it happens, whatever it is, I know I'll get through it." This is the mindset of prevention. But you might think "Nothing's happened, so why bother thinking about prevention? What's there to prevent?" But while this approach might work with your car, it seldom helps your relationships.

When you're aware of the boy's vulnerabilities, you approach emotional situations with a mindset of prevention. Prevention means you've done enough OJT work to know where feelings come from and to whom they belong. When you're vigilant of the boy, and the taxicabs, suitcases, and bullet trains, and how you tend to defend yourself from pain, you have greater confidence. And confidence means more hope for future possibilities.

EXERCISE 9: PREVENTION

1. Ask your partner, friends, and coworkers about your approach or mindset in dealing with change. Or simply reread your earlier progress notes.

2. Ask your partner, friends, or coworkers what you could have done differently in the past to get a better outcome.
3. Look for any patterns in the responses people give you, and also look for patterns in your thoughts and feelings. Are different people telling you the same thing? Are you having the same feeling over and over again?
4. Freely associate, and write down whatever comes to mind. If the boy comes into view, imagine being with him. See what he needs from you. This can clarify why you approach emotional situations the way you do.

PREPARATION

The work you've been doing up to now has helped you make a shift in how you view your life and relationships. You're more in touch with your feelings, thoughts, and reactions, and you're learning how to change your responses that trigger difficult emotions. In OJT terminology, you've been revising your personal blueprint for life.

In this approach to life, you are mindful of the potential for change in emotional situations. For example, instead of expecting a certain outcome when you come home from a hard day at the office, you would realize that your family may not react the way you expect, but will instead be responding to whatever happened in their own lives during the day.

When you're prepared, you're mindful that emotional situations are inevitable, that they happen at random, and that you may not understand what's going on. You also are mindful that the other person wants your help, and that although at first you may have no idea how you can help, you'll find a way to do it.

Being prepared means knowing that the potential for emotional struggles exists, virtually everywhere, and then building this awareness into your daily life, like going to work.

During my work as an engineer, I learned about "Elson's law," a modification of Murphy's law originated by an engineer named Ed Elson from California: "Anything that can go wrong already has, you're just not aware of it yet." This was my working premise as an engineer. It worked then, and it still works. In the counseling room, for example, I know that there is often more to my clients' lives than my clients or I recognize.

Still, I know that there's potential for my clients to have random feelings, and I prepare them for having good and bad experiences that are common in self-improvement work. I help them prepare for feeling the highs and lows that normally accompany the guided imagery they use to visit the boy or their parents or someone else. I prepare them for the likelihood that neither they nor I may understand the events in their boyhood that left them unfulfilled. I prepare them for the likelihood that, by working together in counseling, and later, doing their OJT on their own, they can heal their pain and have a more fulfilling life. I help them realize that their partner's experience in the relationship is different from theirs, but that, like them, she also wants fulfillment and better relationships too. With continued OJT, you too can develop this same mindset of preparation. It's like learning to ride a bicycle. Once you learn how, you never forget.

EXERCISE 10: REPLACING OLD PATTERNS

This exercise compares your old with your changing approaches to emotional situations, and takes about thirty minutes to complete. You can repeat this exercise at any point in this book, to check your progress. There are two ways to do this exercise:

1. Read though your progress notes and look for notes indicating your previous approaches to emotional situations. Uncover your boyhood patterns. On a separate sheet of paper, create two columns with the headings "then" and "now." In the "then" column, list your early approaches to emotional situations before doing OJT. In the "now" column, write what you are better able to do now.

2. Alternately, read the list in the "now" column in the example that follows, and circle the statements that could apply to your life (note that the "now" column reflects a mindset of preparation). On a separate piece of paper, write down how you would have responded before getting this far into OJT. If you have a hard time describing your earlier approaches, read the list in the "then" column, and circle or modify those that are familiar to you.

Then	Now
I'd get angry when asked how I felt.	I know that talking about feelings isn't easy.
I didn't care what she thought.	I try to understand her.
I wanted a drink when I got home.	I think before I drink.
I'd use porn when everyone was asleep.	This urge to use is less, now that we talk.
I felt miserable, no matter what I did.	I wonder if I've been depressed.
I thought, why date? It will just be the same.	I know that I tend to set up my relationships so they fail.

I couldn't commit to relationships.	I tell her if I get afraid she'll leave.
I would do whatever it took.	I'll do all I can, and it may still not be enough.
My kids made me angry.	I think to myself, what's bothering the kids?
She felt like my roommate.	I'd ask myself, have I been distant too?
I didn't trust people.	I still hesitate to trust, but give people the benefit of my doubt.
I hated being lied to.	I ask myself, why would she need to lie?

Doing this exercise shows you how your OJT work can affect your approach to emotional situations. For instance, you can identify times you were a fixer or when you tried to repair a situation or when you used a particular pattern. By comparing "then" and "now" you can gauge your self-improvement and identify those emotional situations that are still difficult for you.

BE PREPARED

In my counseling office, I have a few small sculptures of men holding infants in their arms and holding the hands of small children. When clients ask about these sculptures, I tell them that they symbolize my preparation for the inevitable cries of children in my adult clients. That while I won't immediately know the child's needs, I'm prepared.

Similarly for you, preparation means knowing that the child in you and the child in your partner will, sooner or later, cry for help. How you respond to these two imaginary children and to your adult partner will determine how happy or how miserable you will be.

Now, it's time to give the changes you've made some traction.

Chapter 6
Getting Traction in Your Relationship

Think of this chapter as another OJT bridge-building activity. This imaginary bridge, instead of connecting you to your history, can improve your connection to your current partner or help you with a new relationship. To do this job, you'll continue to use your imagination and you'll apply some of the ideas from the guided imagery work you did in chapter 4. You'll also apply what you learned in chapter 5 about how to respond to emotionally difficult situations.

This chapter encourages you to think of your primary relationship in terms of developmental stages, like the developmental stages of a very young child, and that you and your partner are parenting this child together. When you think of your relationship with your partner in these terms, you can understand the need to nurture it, just as you would a young child. This chapter will focus on how your relationship can develop and mature through your attentive parenting. By the end of this chapter, you'll have a greater understanding of what you need to contribute, emotionally, to your relationship.

This chapter focuses on new and on young relationships, that is, those that are younger than about three years. Nevertheless, if you apply your imagination and creativity, you'll see how the ideas in this chapter can also help if you're in a more mature relationship or if you're rebuilding your current relationship or if you're starting over again after a break-up. This chapter concludes with an imagery exercise that will introduce you to the work you'll do in chapter 7. (For editorial purposes only, in the following sections your partner's gender is assumed to be female.)

<u>RELATIONSHIP MINDSETS</u>

Thinking in terms of relationship *stages* and relationship *parenting* can be helpful when you're learning to think about your responsibilities to your relationship, or understanding the role you have and what you need to contribute.

A new, or "infant," relationship, of about six months or less, has the developmental needs of an actual infant of the same age. If you think about the needs of an infant of this age, you'll have a rough idea of what your primary responsibility is—knowing what you need to provide emotionally so that your relationship can develop and mature during this early period. Likewise, if you've been in an ongoing relationship for about two or three years, and you imagine it's in the "toddler" stage of development, you'll have a rough idea of what the relationship requires from you, emotionally, in order for it to develop and mature during this stage.

All of this is to say that young relationships need parenting. In a new relationship, your role is similar to the role of a new father. When you look at your relationship this way, you lower your risk of making a wrong assumption. For example, in a new relationship, you wouldn't be thinking to yourself, "I thought she'd know that about me by now." Likewise, you wouldn't have unrealistic expectations of yourself, thinking "She'll expect me to know what she wants when I call about this weekend," or feeling ashamed when you do call and she doesn't like your suggestions. In a toddler relationship, you'd be okay with your partner feeling comfortable about venturing outside the relationship, without you, to pursue her own interests, and you'd expect the same comfort in yourself if you wanted to pursue an interest. You'd naturally feel anxious about this at first, like a toddler's father watching his child climb the stairs alone for the first time. But as a good parent, you wouldn't want to get in the way.

STARTING A NEW RELATIONSHIP

If you're in a new relationship or you're thinking about starting one, review exercise 2 in chapter 4, when you imagined being with an infant, and reread your progress notes from that exercise. This review of what an infant needs can help you gauge what you'll need to contribute in your new relationship.

Meeting your partner and starting a new relationship is similar to the birth of a new baby. Usually, an unborn baby is safe and secure inside the mother's womb, and dependent only on the immediate environment for everything it needs. In a similar way, just before you met each other, you and your partner were probably safe and secure, relying mostly on yourselves and your environment to supply your needs.

Then, after meeting your partner and feeling connected to her, your relationship began to take on a life of its own. In time, when your connection developed into a loving bond, your relationship was "born." And when this happened, like the baby leaving the womb, life changed for you and your partner. The "infant" had arrived. Then, like the baby relying on its caretakers for everything, in your newborn relationship, you both started relying on each other for your primary emotional needs—care, nurturing, and love.

Parents of a firstborn tend to be anxious, excited, and a bit jumpy in the beginning since they don't have much experience. If you were a new dad and you heard your baby crying, you probably wouldn't instinctively know what to do, but you would know that your baby was fragile. Whatever you did, you'd do it gently. And, when your efforts to soothe the baby actually calmed it down, you'd realize that not knowing what to do was okay, and that all you needed to do, and all you are responsible for doing, is to care, be gentle, and be attentive. You wouldn't respond to the baby's cries as though he knew better than to cry, and you wouldn't complain to him, scare him, hit him, or scream, drink, or put your child in harm's way when he needed you.

Now, apply this mindset to your infant relationship and your role as a new dad (uncertain, excited, sometimes clumsy), and you'll have a rough idea of what you're responsible for providing (love, care, and attention), and you'll have a good idea of how to respond (with love, care, and attention). You'll know that, like new parents, neither you nor your partner will automatically know what to do, so expect that she also can feel uncertain and be a little clumsy early on.

The father of a new baby normally likes to talk about his excitement and often calls home several times a day to check in on his new family member. So, like a new dad who's full of joy and excitement, don't push aside your desire to celebrate your new relationship. Begin telling people how you feel. And don't forget to tell your partner! Phoning her once or twice a day and letting her know you've been thinking about her will take you about ten to twenty seconds. Like a steel reinforcing rod, this single act can strengthen your new relationship. Just ask your partner.

Like bringing a new baby home from the hospital, a new relationship in your life usually means you'll be doing a lot of adjusting (not surrendering) to your partner's ideas, her habits, her quirks, and her favorite whatever. And you'll be asking your partner to do the same for you. This adjustment takes time and hard work. There's no way around this, so learn how to reach agreements or learn to agree to disagree, peacefully, without hurting or scaring her.

Regardless of how long you're together, you'll never be able to read each other's minds. Early on, develop a habit of asking questions about what your partner would like to have, and what she needs and what she expects. Then work on making these kinds of questions part of your normal communication. And, since your partner can't read your mind either, don't expect her to know what you're thinking. You can encourage her to ask you questions and you can be a good role model by asking her questions about what she thinks. So check in with your partner regularly to ensure you're not getting your exercise by jumping to conclusions. Again, this is all part of a daily process of building better relationships and feeling fulfilled.

TRUST

Trust in a relationship is as vital to moving ahead safely as good tires are crucial to your car's traction. Without trust, your relationship is vulnerable to skidding and going flat. Developing trust in a relationship takes time, just like it does for a baby to develop trust in his caretakers.

Usually, an infant develops trust during about the first six months of life, provided his caretakers feed the baby a steady diet of love, care, and attention. When trust is established, the baby begins to thrive, emotionally and psychologically. The baby develops a secure attachment to his parents, and begins indicating this attachment by spontaneously smiling and making eye contact. If this basic trust never develops, the baby becomes vulnerable to depression, and in severe cases, the child loses interest in and emotionally detaches from his caretakers. Later, when intimacy, friendships, and business require this same person, as an adult, to trust other people, and he can't, he can become trapped in depression and fear.

So, according to the mindset of relationship stages, if a baby needs six months to develop basic trust in his parents, plan on your new relationship needing about the same length of time for trust between you and your partner to gain traction. Learn to be patient. If your partner discloses to you that she's anxious about trust in your relationship, you can gently reassure her that you're mindful of her anxiety and that you'll be there to reassure her often.

Together, you can realize that having basic trust in your relationship doesn't mean that either of you has illusions about your trust being total or absolute. Instead, each of you accepts that basic or "good enough" trust in your relationship is all that you can expect and that this trust can still be violated or fail from time to time. A small boy's basic trust in his parents creates a sense of safety in him—that their love and protection will continue—even though he gets angry at them when he's punished.

When a baby begins spontaneously smiling at his parents, this is evidence that a warm attachment is underway, as though the infant were building a bridge to his parents and the parents are helping. Similarly, you'll feel the trust and attachment building and the bond deepening in your relationship as it's happening. A good indication that basic trust is building is when you can successfully work through tough emotional challenges together, perhaps with sadness, regret, or disappointment, but without emotional pain and suffering.

Like new parents enjoying watching their baby, this early period in your new relationship is a time for pleasure, fun, learning, and exploring your new world together. Like a baby reacting to the sounds of his environment, you'll learn a new language—the language of your relationship—and neither of you will communicate this way with anyone else. You'll develop new mannerisms too, or special ways of being together, that are unique to you as a couple.

As the relationship picks up speed, like a baby learning to crawl, you'll need to be alert for the times your partner needs, or you need, reassurance. There will probably be times when she'll want you simply to listen to whatever she has to say and not do anything. There will probably be times too when she's upset and doesn't know why. These moments normally happen in intimate relationships. If this happens in your relationship, remember that you're not responsible for reading your partner's mind. But you are responsible for regularly reassuring her that you're there to listen, even when you're clueless about why she's upset, for you know that sometimes she can't help but be afraid. All of this attentiveness to your partner is a part of parenting your relationship.

Early on, plan to react with the same comfort you'd give to a small child who's afraid of the dark, because until trust builds, there may be instances when your partner's afraid and won't be able to put her fear into words that you'll understand. Ask your partner about her fears. If you're not in a relationship, ask others you know who are in a newer relationship about this.

Here's a small sample of some fears your partner may have early on in your relationship:

- "Will he leave?"
- "Will I want to leave?"
- "Will either of us lose interest?"
- "Will he cheat?"
- "Is he still attracted to me?"
- "Does he wish he was still single?"

Now, if you're a logical thinker, your partner's fears probably won't make sense to you, but to her, these fears are valid, and how you respond to her when she's afraid means everything to her. Feelings are neither right or wrong, so, at a time like this, ignore your need for logic. Learn to think about your partner's fear like you would think about a child who's had a bad dream. This makes remembering to ask "How can I help?" easy for you to do.

In many emotional situations, especially those involving your partner's fear, you'll feel like you're being handed a cloud. Here's an example of this:

You: "What's wrong?"

Her: "Can't you see? The problem is that I'm afraid!"

You: "How can I help?"

Her: "Help me not be afraid."

You: "What can I do?"

Her: "I don't know!"

There's no logic or reason, nothing you can grab hold of or see, in this exchange. There's only her emotion. At times like this, it's not what you do that's important, but rather, it's how you *are* that can mean everything to the relationship. So, in emotional situations, bear in mind the little girl who's inside your partner, and remember that your gentle reassurance and embrace are often all she may want.

Lastly, in a new relationship, it's a good idea to prepare yourself for most things not going according to your plans. Here you can apply what you learned in chapter 5 about responding to emotionally challenging situations. The best mindset here ranges between preparation and prevention. Be aware that if you insist on being a "fixer" who shuts down feelings, your relationship may not make it to the next stage.

Befor moving on to the next stage, it's worth mentioning that in rare cases, an unknown or forgotten-about childhood trauma may appear, out of the blue, in an adult relationship. While the chance of this happening in your relationship is probably very small, you should nevertheless be familiar with what can happen.

WRECKAGE

Approximately one out of every four women, and about one out of every six men, has been physically and/or sexually abused as a child. Let's look at how this can affect the victim's adult relationship.

When a child is violated, this experience is often pushed into unconscious storage in "My Family History," and later in life, these feelings can come rushing back. This can happen, for instance, in the safety of an adult relationship. Assuming the victim is a woman, the love she feels in the here-and-now can lead to free association, but she cannot always choose which of her little girl experiences will arrive via her taxicabs and bullet trains. Just as a man's association to hurtful boyhood experiences can arrive unexpectedly in the here-and-now, a woman's hurtful childhood experiences may appear without warning in her loving adult relationship. If her suitcases contain the horror of early trauma, and these open in the here-and-now, the victim can react as though it were happening all over again. And in extreme instances, the woman can imagine her partner is the abuser.

Sometimes the presence of children can trigger this. Let's say this woman becomes a parent. When her child reaches about the same age she was when she was violated, her associations to her childhood can reawaken the old pain, and suddenly "now" feels like "then."

Even without early physical trauma, unresolved childhood rage and pain can appear in the here-and-now. For instance, when a parent gives a child the love he or she didn't get as a child, old hurt feelings can arise unexpectedly. This reaction to caring for a child can startle both partners.

Regardless of how it surfaces, if traumatic pain from an early, intimate relationship is stored in either your or your partner's "My Family History," it can impact your adult relationship. So, if you suspect that a serious trauma of any kind is in your or your partner's histories, you may want to talk to a qualified professional.

UP AND RUNNING: TWO TO THREE YEARS LATER

If you're in a "toddler" relationship, recall exercise 3 in chapter 4, when you imagined being with a toddler, and reread your progress notes from that exercise. This review, and thinking about your relationship in terms of stages and parenting, can help you gauge what you'll need to contribute to your relationship. If you and your partner can picture your relationship as a toddler, it will be easier for you both to accept the many changes that can happen around this time.

Parents can tell you about situations they never imagined would happen, that is, until their baby became a toddler. The same might be said about a young relationship; despite having basic trust, you won't always know what will happen next or how your relationship will develop. Each of you need enough time, from about your second to your third year together, of playing side-by-side and living together, in order for both of you to feel securely attached in the relationship. Learn to tolerate and be prepared for emotional highs and lows in your relationship as this attachment develops. You won't always be in synch with your partner, and this is natural. Be prepared too for out-of-the-blue experiences, just as the toddler's parents are prepared during the so-called terrible twos.

Also, according to our building code, as intimacy builds and you're each feeling safer and more secure, you'll probably experience parts of your partner's "My Family History" you had no idea were there. Old baggage may still get in the way. Learn to be patient, and be aware that your partner may need your encouragement to stay patient too. Since playing together can soften the anxiety in your relationships, you can help your toddler relationship mature by suggesting playful activities or by responding to your partner's playfulness.

Learning more about the child in each of you can have pleasant side effects. For example, your creativity as a couple can begin to flourish as you think spontaneously of things you can do together. Your relationship not only has its own style of communication, but, like a toddler, it may seem to develop its own personality. For instance, sometimes people will refer to the two of you as one, and this can feel great.

In these early few years, avoid setting too many restrictions on your imagination or your partner's imagination. Share your fantasies about a future together. This playfulness and imagining helps prepare you for times when your relationship may lose traction and start to skid. Trust, imagination, and playfulness allow you to invent your own solutions to problems, together. Mutual creativity can bring hope back to your relationship in difficult times, so do all you can to encourage mutual thinking outside the box.

EXERCISE 11: GETTING TO KNOW YOU

Ever wonder how well your partner really knows you? Your partner probably asks herself the same question. One way of showing your partner that she matters to you is to pay attention to her likes and dislikes. To gauge how well your partner would say you know her, try answering the following questions.

1. What is your partner's deepest fear?
2. In what ways is your partner most vulnerable?
3. What do you know about your partner's childhood?

4. Did your partner survive childhood trauma?
5. Would your partner say "He really hears what I say"?
6. In what ways does your partner nurture herself?
7. Is your partner bored or confused in the relationship with you?
8. Name your partner's favorite
    - color
    - fragrance
    - flower
    - piece of jewelry
    - song
    - movie
    - actor
    - author
    - time of year
    - thing about you
    - sexual fantasy

After answering the above, show your list of answers to your partner and see which ones you got right. Alternatively, you can do this exercise together, by each making up a list of questions for each other.

Like the toddler exploring his little world, partners often begin exploring their own interests apart from each other at about this stage. When you or your partner venture out to explore more of life, one of you may feel left behind. So, if you begin exploring, for example, a business venture, remember that she may be vulnerable to feeling abandoned. And if she ventures out, you might associate to your boyhood, and if you felt left behind then, you might feel this way again. Remember to always tell your partner how you're feeling and what you need, modeling for her how she can do the same.

A toddler needs to feel important to his parents. Parents nurture their toddler by paying attention to him. This is why your partner wants you to "see" the relationship, to respect it (like remembering important dates, how you met each other, and where you went on your first date), and to recognize what's special about the two of you together.

Men who nurture their relationship in the ways discussed in this chapter can more easily build and maintain a connection to their partner. As you nurture your relationship in its early stages, your relationship will grow stronger. The last part of this book will focus on helping you access the five natural abilities that you have for personal fulfillment. Like so many men, you may have lost track of what these abilities are, because of life's many distractions and demands.

Before moving on to chapter 7, please do the following exercise.

EXERCISE 12: CONSOLIDATION

You will need about thirty minutes of uninterrupted quiet for this imagery exercise, and it's preferable that you do the exercise in your living room at home. If you can't be in your home, imagine that you're there when you do the exercise. No other preparations are necessary. If you have the urge to write at any point, just go ahead with it. If you're resistant or have uncomfortable feelings or other reactions at any point, pause briefly and refer to chapter 2 or to the websites in the introduction for help with this. Now you are ready to take the following steps.

Look around the room you're in, and take a mental inventory of everything you see, like the furniture, pictures on the walls, rugs, curtains, TV, decorations, and the other items in the room. Next, imagine that today is moving day, and you're moving out of this home, into a new home that's located in a neighborhood you've always admired. Your new home has the same floor plan as your current home. To help you feel at home as soon as you can, you'll first move all the furnishings of the room you're sitting in and arrange these furnishings as you like in the new living room. The furniture from the remaining rooms will be moved later.

Next, picture a moving van outside your current home, and imagine that you're able to move everything yourself. Then, imagine driving away from your home. Take as long a road trip as you'd like in your imagination as you drive to your new home. Picture yourself driving up to your new home and parking at the curb. See yourself walking up to the front door and finding a notice pinned to the door, listing the following five things you must do, in order to move in:

1. You must bring all the living room furnishings from the moving van into your new home. You cannot leave any items outside.
2. You must place all of these furnishings in your new living room.
3. You must decorate this room alone, using only your ideas and the furnishings you brought.
4. Even though your new home has the same floor plan as your old home, you cannot decorate this room the way it was decorated in your old home. Nothing can face in the same direction or be in the same place as before.
5. Expect visitors.

Like most moving-in jobs, imagine this job starts with everything piled in the middle of your new living room. Staying mindful of the five conditions for moving in, use your imagination to come up with different arrangements for the new living area. Picture yourself moving the furnishings around a few times, looking for an arrangement that you'd like to live in and one that you'd feel comfortable showing to your guests. It may help you to make a few sketches in your progress notes of the different arrangements.

For example, could you place the furniture in a way that would encourage your guests to converse rather than encourage them to watch the TV? How could you arrange the furniture to make TV-watching an option? Could you arrange the lamps so the room appears brighter, or do you want to create a romantically lit corner? How could you place the cushions and rugs to make the room look warmer or more open? How could you place the wall hangings and knick-knacks to make the room cozier or to show off certain objects? When you've selected an arrangement that meets conditions 1 through 4, spend a few minutes imagining yourself relaxing in this new home, and notice how you feel in your body as you picture this scene.

Now, make an imaginary transition, and imagine that, collectively, these furnishings symbolize everything about you as a person, as a friend, and as a relationship partner. So, when your imaginary guests arrive, this new arrangement of the symbolic furnishings will convey your true personality, your character, your ability to maintain your relationships, your playfulness, and your self-esteem. In other words, the imaginary furnishings reflect your inner self, and now, in your new home, you have the best of you, and perhaps the not-so-best of you, on display, and your guests can immediately see who you really are.

Perhaps the fireplace represented your intensity in your old home, and, because of how you had placed the furniture, visitors had to sit near the fire, where they'd mistake your intensity for anger. In your new home, the fireplace still represents your intensity, but the new furniture arrangement allows guests to sit at a comfortable distance from the heat. As a result, the fire evenly warms the room, conveying a sense of welcome. In your new home, you've placed your favorite easy chair out in the open, so your visitors can see you're able to relax. Still, by leaving the chair's wear and tear visible, you let your guests know the truth—you can't always relax. And they can see that you've sat alone many times, stressed and afraid, and aren't afraid to let others know that you struggle.

Unlike your old home, you've arranged the furniture so that your guests can move about easily. From wherever they're standing, they're able to see and hear each other. Your guests recognize that this new arrangement displays your willingness to communicate. In your old home, you used the coffee and end tables to keep others away from you; in your new home you've opened up the room and made it easier for guests to approach you. Continue with this imagery until you've connected the different pieces of furniture and decor in this new arrangement to different parts of yourself. Taking notes and making a sketch or two to keep track of these associations can help.

Now, you may want to look at those pieces of furniture (or parts of yourself) that you'd like to refurbish, that is, the parts of you that you'd like to change. For example, you may be bothered by the fact that your favorite chair isn't looking too comfortable lately. Although the wear and tear shows your guests the toll that stress and worry have had on your comfort, perhaps you'd like to have the chair reupholstered. You'd like not to worry and stress as much as you do. And the coffee and end tables are scratched and chipped, displaying to your guests how you've kept others away from you, and now you admit you want this part of your life to change. Now imagine that these changes take place. Now, everything in your new home is just the way you want it. You can also note which pieces of furniture or parts of yourself you've kept hidden. Most everyone has these pieces as well.

Now, imagine that once you've rearranged everything, touched up chipped paint, refurbished worn parts, you're feeling more comfortable, more at home with everything about you. You like what you see and hope for a knock at the door.

WHAT JUST HAPPENED?

By reading the exercise, letting your imagination create pictures, and letting your body feel any sensations that arise, you may begin to realize or more clearly understand a basic truth about human life—like most people, you already have within you all that you need to feel fulfilled and to build better relationships. This imaginary move illustrates how it's possible to rearrange your internal world, so life feels better, using only what you already have. Personal fulfillment and better relationships are possible when you

- know and think about what you already have, that is, your personal abilities
- rearrange, or make accessible, what you have
- repair the abilities that are misplaced or worn
- put away what's harmful until you can get rid of it.

Lasting internal change means both knowing and thinking about your internal world and how you can rearrange it, so you are comfortable. In chapter 7, you'll learn more about your basic internal furniture and the existing parts of yourself that you may not think about. These are the parts that hundreds of wives, girlfriends, and daughters talk to me about when they describe what they need from their men to feel connected, valued and respected.

Self-improvement is a remodeling job. While you can't rewrite your history, through self-understanding and self-exploration, you can change how it affects your life today. All you need is what you have, right here, right now.

PAUSE

It's time to rest. Please stop here and sit with your feelings for about five to ten minutes. This means that you allow your feelings to surface, and you let your mind's eye show you the images that are linked to your feelings. As this happens, or soon afterward, write about your feelings, what you see, and your associations. If you feel anxious, refer to chapter 2 or to the websites in the introduction.

Chapter 7
Personal Fulfillment

The capacity for personal fulfillment lies within each of us, and this capacity is normally available from boyhood on. However, if you grew up in a difficult or uncaring family environment, the energy you put into coping with your situation used up the emotional energy that you needed to be a fun-loving kid.

This would have happened, for example, if one or both of your parents were too depressed or too drunk or too disorganized to fulfill their role as parents. You may have had to do things that they were responsible for doing, like cook the family meals, manage the house, shop for groceries, and take care of your siblings. If either of your parents were prone to violence or intimidation, you would have learned to develop strategies to safeguard yourself and your siblings. If you lived in a situation like this, you would have put your boyhood feelings, along with your hopes and dreams, aside, and in the process, you would have lost track of how to feel fulfilled as a kid.

Luckily, you still have the capacity to feel fulfilled, even if you've lost access to it. This capacity is mixed in with your boyhood experiences in the storeroom of your unconscious mind called "My Family History." The OJT work you've been doing has helped clear away some of the painful experiences in this storeroom so that you can reconnect with this innate capacity and bring it into the here-and-now.

This capacity breaks down into five natural abilities that we all have—to feel, to communicate, to tell the truth, to understand ourselves, and to play. You were born with these abilities, even if they have fallen into disuse. For example, telling the truth today may not be easy to do if you learned to lie in order to survive in the family. Being playful can be difficult if you seldom smiled as a boy, and it can be hard to communicate after decades of living in fear and silence.

In other words, unresolved boyhood experiences that hurt and confused you have been obstacles that blocked or interfered with your access to these natural abilities. With OJT and bridge building, you have cleared away these obstacles and reopened your routes to fulfillment. In this final chapter, you'll take a journey along each one of these routes. Doing the exercises will help you gauge how much access you have to each ability—to feel, to tell the truth, to understand yourself, to communicate, and to play—and help you identify what needs further work.

Think of these exercises as if you were applying the last coat of pavement to your bridge's roadway, painting the bright yellow lines that define each lane. This work will take you about two to three hours to complete, so choose a comfortable environment, such as the one you used in earlier exercises. (For editorial purposes only, in these exercises your partner's gender is assumed to be female.)

ACCESSING YOUR ABILITY TO FEEL

How many times has someone asked you, "How are you?" And how many times do you say "Everything's great" when you're not okay? At times, such as when you're at work, this response is appropriate. But in your closest relationship, you need to express your true feelings to reinforce your connection and build trust between you and your partner.

Emotions are part of the human experience (they're almost like having a sixth sense), so why are they so difficult for so many of us to talk about? Here are three possible reasons why you may have a hard time expressing your emotions.

1. You're not sure how you feel.

If you're generally confused about how you feel when you're in an emotional situation, this pattern probably began when you were a young boy. For example, if your parents blamed you for making them feel bad because you were sad or hurt or angry, the message you received was "It's better not to have such feelings." Or maybe they told you that you were too sensitive or that you acted like a girl when you expressed your feelings. Maybe they told you that what you were feeling was wrong. In a loving or close adult relationship, these experiences would arrive in taxicabs or bullet trains, and as you'd struggle to describe your feelings, your partner or the other person would get confused too.

2. You know how you feel, but you're too embarrassed or ashamed to discuss it.

Feeling ashamed or embarrassed in emotional situations as a boy and not having loving parents to help you understand this can lead to a pattern of shame in adult relationships. Your family may have ridiculed you for talking about your feelings. Or, if you shared your feelings with your family, you may have felt awkward afterward because their emotional coldness conveyed that your feelings didn't matter.

Now, in your closest relationships, you become embarrassed or ashamed when your friends or your partner asks you how you feel about your relationship with them. Your partner may get angry if she thinks, "He's ashamed to be with me!" Or, you may avoid women altogether because you're embarrassed about feeling inadequate.

Shame is a powerful and sometimes painful emotion and often a precursor to destructive reactions, like alcohol and food binges, addictions to work, sex and internet pornography, and drug abuse. I drank for decades to numb the shame I felt since boyhood, and I was able to imagine stopping drinking only when I admitted to myself and to others how ashamed I felt.

3.   You know what you feel, and you wish you could express your emotions, but the boy's fear is too great.

If fear usually stops you from saying how you feel in emotional situations, this probably began when you were a boy. For example, your parents would get angry at you for expressing your feelings or for simply wanting to be a fun-loving, spontaneous kid. Maybe they'd say something like "Children are supposed to be seen and not heard—or else!" Now, when feelings well up inside of you and you want to express them, a taxicab delivers a suitcase full of panic. This fear—and the damage it can cause—isn't limited to an emotional situation at home. For example, you avoid constructive debates at work, because disagreements leave you anxious, and by doing this, you hurt your career.

Whatever the reason, when you avoid your true feelings, your situation can get worse. When you don't express your feelings, you usually will have other feelings that are more distressing than those feelings you've been avoiding, and you put yourself at risk.

Expressing your feelings is an innate ability. You were born with this ability. When you were about three months old, your parents could tell when you were happy or sad or angry or distressed or disgusted or startled, simply by your facial expressions. And when you were able to speak, you had the ability to express your basic feelings, like being sad, mad, happy, or afraid. This ability was also natural. This next exercise will help you recognize feelings you've had since boyhood and will help you recognize feelings you have now.

EXERCISE 13: EXAMINING YOUR FEELINGS

First, review the following list of natural feelings

abandonment	envy	jealousy
anger	fear	joy
annoyance	fulfillment	loneliness
anxiety	grief	love
being lost	guilt	numbness
boredom	hate	playful
confidence	helplessness	rage
confusion	hopelessness	regret
depression	hurt	resentment
detachment	inadequacy	sadness
emptiness	isolation	shame

Next, please gather together a small group of photos and/or a few home videos or movies that were taken when you were a boy. These can be from any time up to your late teenage years. If these are unavailable, you can refer to your progress notes from exercises 1 through 4 in chapter 4, or you can simply repeat the initial imagery part of any of those four exercises to reconnect with the boy at any age.

Next, look closely into the boy's eyes in each photo or video or image, and notice his facial expressions. As you look at each image of the boy, answer the following questions in your notebook. Refer back to the feelings listed above.

- What do you remember about yourself and your family at that time?
- How do you imagine the boy in the picture or video or image was feeling?
- How do you imagine the others in the picture or video or image felt?
- What feelings or associations or reactions are you having now?
- Are you willing to share these with anyone? Why? Why not?

PAUSE:

It's time to rest. Please stop here. During this pause it's important that you sit with your feelings for five to ten minutes. This means that you allow your feelings to surface, and you let your mind's eye show you the images that are linked to this feeling. As this happens, or soon afterward, write about how you feel, what you see, and your associations. If you feel anxious, refer to chapter 2 or to the websites in the introduction.

Close your eyes if you can, and focus on the experience of being able to feel what life was like in your family. Feel your ability to feel. Repeat this process as many times as you wish. The boy will enjoy your company.

In this next part of this exercise, please recall a recent time when you didn't understand what you were feeling, or a time when you didn't understand why you were feeling a certain way, or a time when you struggled with expressing how you were feeling. (You can use imagery to help you recall these times.) Then answer the following questions:

1. What were your thoughts and feelings at that time? Refer to the earlier list of feelings for help with this.

2. Imagine returning to the situation. What could you say to yourself that would be comforting and that would help you to express your feelings? Please pause here for about five to ten minutes, and think about your answer. Rest; close your eyes. Compare what you actually did in the situation before you understood your feelings, to what you can imagine doing now if the same situation arose. How would you respond? How would you feel? Notice how much more you're able to feel.

3. Can you identify any thoughts and feelings that you're having now that are similar to your reactions to the photos or videos or the images from the previous part of this exercise? Please pause here for about five to ten minutes. Rest; close you eyes, and think about your answer. If you answered yes, you've identified a strong association to the boy: it will help to write about this in your progress notes.

Before continuing, imagine for a moment that from here forward, your ability to feel will be available to you at any time, anywhere. Now, to keep the promise you made to the boy in chapter 4 (if you haven't done so already), imagine being with him and letting him know you're thinking about him, as you said you would, and let him know how you're feeling—he'll enjoy hearing about it.

ACCESSING YOUR ABILITY TO BE TRUTHFUL

A boy usually learns about the meaning and value of truthfulness through his early family interactions. Then, before applying what he learns in his little world, the boy must sense that telling the truth won't bring him harm or harm his family. Under these conditions and knowing about normal consequences, like restrictions or being grounded, many boys still tell the truth.

If, however, by telling the truth, there's a risk of damaging his relationship with his parents or there's a risk of harming his parents' relationship, a boy may give more priority to the relationships and less priority to the truth. A boy who associates truth with harm becomes like a little soldier, developing strategies so he can maneuver around the truth. Eventually strategies and manipulation becomes his life's highway, while his access to the truth becomes a narrow and difficult path.

In the exercises in chapter 4, when you imagined yourself holding the infant or sitting with the toddler or talking to the teenage boy, it's doubtful you thought about lying to the boy or that you imagined that the boy lied to you. And when you imagined your parents as children, you probably weren't lying to them and they weren't lying to you. In fact, spending time with the boy and with your parents as children often revives how truthfulness feels at the deepest level of your experience.

This is why this book repeatedly recommends that you connect with the boy on a regular basis, because in these images, you reestablish access to your truthfulness. Furthermore, each time you talk with your partner about the boy, each time you tell your partner what you're afraid will happen if you tell the truth, and each time you clarify your intentions, you reinforce your ability for truthfulness.

EXERCISE 14: ACCESSING THE TRUTH

1. Repeat any one of the exercises from chapter 4.
2. After these images fade away, write down a lie you can remember telling. The lie that comes to mind first is the one you're looking for, and it doesn't matter when you lied. What matters is that you still remember it, and that you might still have some discomfort in your body as you remember

it. If there's more than one lie, write down the first one you recall.

3. Write down the price you paid for lying, in terms of your aliveness. For example, did you damage or lose a relationship? Did your reputation suffer? Did your health suffer? Did your self-esteem get worse? How do you feel as you remember telling this lie?

4. Write down the corresponding truth, in its entirety.

5. Imagine going back to this time that you lied and that you could enter this scene. See and hear yourself apologize and telling the person you lied to what you were afraid of that got you to lie.

PAUSE:

It's time to rest. Please stop here. During this pause it's important that you sit with your feelings for five to ten minutes. This means that you allow your feelings to surface, and you let your mind's eye show you the images that are linked to this feeling. As this happens, or soon afterward, write about how you feel, what you see, and your associations. If you feel anxious, refer to chapter 2 or to the websites in the introduction.

CLARIFYING YOUR INTENTIONS

Truthfulness in your relationships starts with identifying what you want, what you're willing to do and not willing to do, and what your personal boundaries are, before the relationship gets underway. This applies to your business relationships, your friendships, your family relationships, and your closest relationship. It helps if you write these things down because you can use what you write as your personal mission statement for the relationship. Once you've identified your wants, needs, and boundaries, it's up to you to communicate your intentions. Remember that no one can read your mind. The following examples illustrate statements of clear intentions.

- "I am committed to this relationship despite our differences."
- "When I lie to her or when I'm tempted to lie to her, I'll get professional help."
- "I won't treat her the way my father treated my mother."
- "I'll stay mindful of the little girl in her."
- "I intend to be a fair father, no matter how badly my child gets into trouble."
- "I won't hire my friends."
- "I'll be her companion but not her husband or the father to her children."
- "I can offer her children my encouragement and friendship, nothing more."
- "I can offer financial backing but not leadership."
- "I can offer her my love and care, but not a commitment."
- "When I say I'll do something, I'll do what I said."
- "My company will operate within the law."
- "I won't lend money to my employees, but I'll help them find a solution."
- "If she's verbally abusive, I'll try to understand, but I won't tolerate it long term."
- "If my employees steal, I will press charges."
- "I don't know how long I will be able to stay. Right now, I don't want to leave."

EXERCISE 15: CURRENT RELATIONSHIPS

Think about a current relationship that you have, such as your closest relationship, your business partnership, or one of your friendships. Write down your intentions using the following four topics and the examples of intentions to guide you:

1. Your short-term (less than three months) and your long-term goals.
2. Your personal limits and boundaries.
3. What you can and can't provide within these limits and boundaries.
4. Your level of commitment.

Now, repeat this process, imagining yourself as if you were the other person. If you're comfortable, share these results with him or her. This usually gets the truth about your relationship out in the open, and then you can work together and clear up any misunderstandings.

CLEARING UP MISUNDERSTANDINGS

Sometimes, misunderstandings or confusion seem like lies. One source of mix-ups is when you try to "mix" one relationship with another relationship. For example, if you develop a friendship and you expect your friend to be your lover as well, your new friend may feel deceived. Likewise, if you want a lover, don't ask your business partner or your client or your patient. If you want a spouse, don't ask her to be your secretary or your mother or your maid.

DEALING WITH TEMPTATION

Lastly, if you're tempted to lie, pause for a moment before saying anything and imagine being with the boy. Then, imagine telling him a lie and notice how you feel. This short process can help clear your thoughts and helps you not only in telling the truth but in telling the other person how hard this is for you. Then the two of you will begin to understand each other better.

ACCESSING YOUR UNDERSTANDING

When you do OJT and learn about what the boy needed and didn't get, you reestablish access to your ability to understand why you think, act, and feel the way you do. With this ability, you can approach life based on your here-and-now needs, instead of trying to meet imaginary needs from your there-and-then. This self-understanding helps you sustain peace of mind in your personal and professional life; others will perceive your newfound self-confidence.

To understand your history means you understand your adult strengths and weaknesses. With this self-understanding, it's much easier to accept the differences between yourself and others and to have realistic expectations of your relationships. Self-understanding helps you appreciate why you want to be with a particular person. When you're able to identify and understand your own needs in a relationship, you're better able to stay aware of your partner's needs. Understanding in a relationship also means that you recognize that your partner is not with you simply to meet your needs.

EXERCISE 16: RATE YOUR DEGREE OF UNDERSTANDING

In this exercise, you'll rate your degree of understanding in a relationship that you're in. Think of an important relationship in your life. Then read each of the eight indicators, or statements, below and rate each one on a scale of 1 to 10, based on how well the statement describes your level of understanding in your relationship.

As an example, look at the first statement: "I assume the other person is not my opponent." In the relationship you're thinking about, if you seldom assume that the other person is your opponent, you'd rate yourself somewhere near the high end of the 1 to 10 scale, say an 8. If you usually assume the other person is your opponent, you'd rate yourself lower, say a 2, for this item. Don't forget to rate each of the indicators below.

INDICATORS

1. "I assume the other person is not my opponent."
2. "I recognize that the other person's experience will be different from mine."
3. "I expect the other person to think, feel and react differently from me."
4. "I remain aware of how I'm feeling."
5. "I'm mindful of the other person's feelings."
6. "I identify as much as I can with the other person's circumstance."
7. "I'm curious about the other person's perspectives."
8. "My first reaction to conflict is tolerance, not winning."

To improve your level of understanding, you can focus your self-improvement efforts on the indicators with lower scores. If you'd like to confirm these estimates, you can ask the other person to review what you wrote down. First pause and make sure that you're comfortable talking to the other person about this exercise and that he or she will be okay with the idea. Then describe the exercise and show the other person your results. You can also use this exercise to identify patterns of misunderstanding in other relationships. If you rate yourself near the high end of the understanding scale for a given statement when others rate you near the low end, you'll know where to focus your self-improvement efforts.

EXERCISE 17: UNDERSTANDING YOUR CURRENT RELATIONSHIP

In this exercise, you'll think about your current romantic partner. If you're not in a romantic relationship at this time, think of a past romantic relationship. Then answer the following:

1. How would you describe her degree of bridge building?
2. Are you able to picture the young girl in her?

3. If so, describe her early family environment.

4. What do you imagine she needs from this relationship?

5. How would you describe her overall feeling about life? For example, is she generally content or doubtful or angry?

6. How do you imagine she truly feels about her relationship with you? For example, is she fulfilled or uncertain or afraid or bored or confused?

7. If you'd like to confirm your answers, pause and make sure you're comfortable talking to her and that she'll be okay with this idea. Then describe this exercise and show her your results.

You may not feel comfortable talking with her about this exercise. Perhaps you had to make assumptions and act on them while you were growing up, especially about your closest relationships. If this is true, you will continue using this pattern as an adult, even with bridge building underway, until you get into the habit of checking out your assumptions. This requires that you communicate.

ACCESSING YOUR ABILITY TO COMMUNICATE

When you were about twelve months old, you probably didn't use clearly understood words to express how you were feeling, but you had the natural ability to communicate. When you had a feeling, like joy or fear, you let people know how you felt, usually through changing your facial expression, which, temporarily, was the "language" you used. Sometimes your parents tried to respond to you using this language and would change their facial expressions.

Parents communicate with their babies nonverbally and verbally. They do this because they're naturally empathic. That is, they're usually so tuned in to their baby that they feel what they imagine their baby is feeling. Although you didn't realize it, you too became tuned in to your parents. For example, if your mother's face showed distress, it would have been normal if you stopped what you were doing and either waited for her facial expression to change or you approached her with a look of concern. If she was routinely distressed or was unresponsive to your concerned look or to your attempts to comfort her, you would become confused about your ability to communicate with her and with others.

All this is to say that each of us has the natural ability to communicate from a very early age. And how well it gets developed depends primarily on what happens to us in our family relationships during the first few years of life. If you were free to express your frustrations as a baby, and your parents responded to you lovingly, then developing your ability to communicate, verbally and nonverbally, would continue. In your toddler years, if your parents responded to your "terrible twos" in a loving and firm way, you'd continue accessing and developing your ability to let them know how you felt and what you wanted.

Bridge building has helped to reestablish your "internal network" of communication, which is made up of your associations, your imagination, your mind's eye, and your internal voice that belongs to the boy. (You can monitor improvements to your internal network by reviewing your progress notes.) Oddly, with OJT, to learn about yourself, you've communicated to yourself about yourself. Once this internal communication is operational, your ability to communicate your feelings to others is also reestablished.

Thinking about my boyhood, the family environment seemed more like a group of soldiers, with each one of us in our own emotional foxholes, clueless about how each other felt and each of us too scared to ask. We focused on survival and usually kept to ourselves. At age thirteen, I began drinking, and when I imagined building a crawl-rope bridge to the adjacent foxhole, this fantasy was soon washed away by alcohol. Twenty years later, when I stopped drinking and using drugs, I regained my desire for fulfillment and got help from someone who knew how to design and build bridges between then and now. In time, I regained access to my capacity for authentic communication, and then relationships with wonderful people became available.

COMMUNICATING IN YOUR RELATIONSHIP

Communication fuels relationships. Without it, the relationship sits by the roadside, unable to move. And like a car without gas, a relationship without good communication is hard to keep pushing. Eventually, people get tired.

Like planning an actual road trip, enjoying a romantic journey or a friendship or a business partnership requires that you pay close attention to the communication fuel gauge. And like putting fuel in your car, your relationship runs better when you fuel it with "high octane" communication—clearly and consistently communicating your feelings and your true intentions.

When you notice that your relationship is getting poor gas mileage, that is, when you're having more disagreements in your relationship, it's important to check the fuel's octane and to put in the right additives if you need to. For example, are you clearly stating your honest intentions or are you using the bargain-priced gasoline of innuendo or assumption?

PAUSE:

It's time to rest. Please stop here. During this pause it's important that you sit with your feelings for five to ten minutes. This means that you allow your feelings to surface, and you let your mind's eye show you the images that are linked to this feeling. As this happens, or soon afterward, write about how you feel, what you see, and your associations. If you feel anxious, refer to chapter 2 or to the websites in the introduction.

EXERCISE 18: UNDERSTANDING ARGUMENTS

This exercise helps you see the flashpoint in an argument, which is usually the moment in time when you or the other person suddenly feels hurt and alone. This is the point when the communication fuel gauge approaches empty and a disagreement becomes an argument.

Think about your current relationship with your romantic partner, or think about another important relationship that relies on clear communication. Recall a time when you argued with your partner or with the other person. Next, imagine walking into this scene as you've done in other exercises in this book, and when you can see yourself being in the argument, answer the following:

1. Recall the sequence of verbal exchanges.
2. Recall what was said that left you feeling alone or angry or hurt.
3. Recall at what point this was said, and recall if you said it.
4. Focus your mind's eye on this moment.
5. Imagine telling the other person how you felt at that moment.
6. Imagine listening to the other person tell you how he or she was feeling at that moment.
7. Imagine talking to the other person about what you will do differently the next time you disagree, and imagine listening to the other person's ideas about this.
8. Notice how you're feeling, emotionally and physically, as you do this exercise.

9. Review your progress notes and look for an example of an earlier situation in which you struggled with communication. Read what you wrote then and imagine what you were thinking and how you were feeling at the time. Next, think through that earlier situation again, and write down how you think and feel about it now. Compare what you wrote today with what you wrote then, and you'll see the improvement in your ability to describe, and therefore to communicate, your thoughts and feelings. Here's an example of such a comparison:

10. <u>Earlier entry</u>: "I just can't get through to her! I get so mad, I can't think straight. All I can think of is having a few drinks."
    <u>Current entry</u>: "It's obvious now that I blamed her whenever we fought, just like my mother blamed me for her bad moods. Reading that entry, it's clear I felt just as helpless when I wrote it as I did when my mother blamed me. I was avoiding fights, hiding behind anger and alcohol, just like I'd overeat as a kid. Now I understand how I replayed the boy's feelings at home and how much I've changed."

With practice, you'll be able to keep your lines of communication open. When you recognize the bullet train arriving with suitcases of pain, and when you can stop to realize that your partner's suitcases are nearby too, you actually have time to refuel the relationship with clear communication and to leave your suitcases unopened. When you and your partner can do this, you might have room to play together.

ACCESSING YOUR PLAYFULNESS

Like your other abilities, your comfort with playfulness now stems from your freedom to play as a child, and if you have access to this ability, you have access to an oasis when your life becomes dry and barren. If you ask women, a lot of them will say they like a playful man, especially early on in a relationship when playfulness helps them feel less anxious.

Small children often communicate what they are thinking or feeling through the language of play, using toys as well as words. This is why children can sometimes seem at peace for extended periods while they play. Usually, playing with your child builds the connection between you and your child, especially when you ask questions about the activity. With you as a regular playmate, your child can develop a sense of being safe in the world.

And like children, when you're a playful adult, people are easily drawn to you. Still, like a lot of other men, you may find that your lightheartedness can get buried beneath the complexities of life, like working two jobs and striving for career advancement and wanting more community involvement and raising a family and coping with financial pressures, and at times, coping with depression. Regaining a sense of playfulness takes work. If you've lost track of this ability, rekindling it takes dedication and focus.

And it's in this spirit that I offer the following suggestions. I hope, as you read along, the boy will show up in your mind's eye, and he'll suggest ways for you to play too.

EXERCISE 19: PLAYING

Start by rating your current ability to play, using a scale of 1 to 10, with 10 as the highest rating and 1 as the lowest rating for your playfulness. Next, select any three play activities from the following list or come up with your own list of three play activities. Do the three activities you've identified as soon as you're able to. Ask your partner to join you, and you can play together.

- Spend time in a toy store and buy the toy or game that leaves you smiling.
- Spend time with children you know and playfully interact with them. Children love to laugh at your funny faces, and they can get most adults to join them in their laughter.
- Visit a kids' sporting event. Pee-wee football and baseball can be great fun to watch.
- Attend a live comedy show or see a funny movie.
- Learn to tell three jokes.
- Take up a hobby.
- Visit an amusement park.
- Give a surprise party.
- Have a potluck dinner party.

When you've done the three activities, rate your playfulness again, and if your partner was with you, have her rate you as a playmate. Did you give yourself a higher number than you did before? Over time, you may find that with practice, playing becomes effortless.

The responsibility for accessing and using your innate abilities is yours alone. It does not belong to your partner, your kids, your boss, or anyone else. No one else is responsible for the quality or outcome of your life. How you partake in it, personally and professionally, is up to you. It's time to stop relying on other people for the quality of your life, if that's what you've done. Mother Nature gave you your five pieces of internal furniture and the responsibility for their upkeep and arrangement.

Keep in mind, the boy is always with you. Now is as good a time as any to act like a kid, perhaps the way you've always wanted to act. Besides, people normally forgive foolishness in a grown man.

Finally, remember that your partner is doing much the same thing you do in life. She too makes associations, finds fulfillment in sitting with her feelings, lives out old patterns of hurtful experiences, tries to find her own way, and has to deal with her incoming taxicabs and bullet trains.

DAILY FULFILLMENT

So here you are at the end of your OJT program. You've built a fabulous bridge between then and now, and it's open for use. But, like any bridge, to keep this bridge open and your traffic moving in both directions you'll have to work at it—every day.

Reading this book (or any other self-improvement book) and doing the work doesn't make you a better partner or give you more fulfillment. This book is just the beginning. To have fulfillment every day, you must commit to keep working on self-improvement. Can you do this? Can you make the daily commitment to do the following?

- Visit the boy.
- Keep progress notes.
- Be truthful.
- Sit with your feelings.
- Clearly communicate your intentions.
- Listen to your partner.
- Be prepared.
- Be playful.
- Deepen your self-understanding.
- Help your partner feel safe and secure.

If so, your life and your relationships will flourish.

I won't lie to you and say that because you've done this work you've become a better partner. I can say that you're aware of the daily process of being a better individual, and you're aware that you'll always have to be doing this work.

The point of bridge building is to own all your feelings, good and bad, especially those that you were told as a boy not to feel. So often we've been brainwashed. But when we make connections with our history, we realize that we have hated, scorned, envied, and deceived, as well as loved and felt fulfillment. We need to question what's important. Is it our toys, our power, or is it fulfillment? If you've grown to think that being "happy" is what's most important, think again, because it's being in intimate contact with your partner and being richly aware of yourself, and not your toys, that leads to personal fulfillment.

Fulfillment in life will arrive and depart each of us every day. But in the final analysis, it's the process of being present regardless of the circumstance that enriches us and leaves us fulfilled. It's not what we achieve or covet that matters. To sustain fulfillment, we must remain present, stay in the moment, feel what needs to be felt, whether it's pain or joy, and attend to our relationships.

In every aspect of your relationships, you must be able to drop into your feelings, into your internal reflective place, every day, and know that tomorrow life will be different from today. Rethink what's important. Is it important for you to feel the pain and the joy with someone you love, or is it the search for the "fool's gold" of "I'll be happy when I have…"?

RIBBON CUTTING

It's time to celebrate! Your bridge is complete. So, picture the construction materials cleared away. You're standing at the head of the crowd, with your here-and-now experiences around you cheering, all eager to make sense. Across the bridge, you see another crowd, your there-and-then experiences, waiting and cheering, anxious to move freely whenever they're needed to make sense of the here-and-now. Imagine a yellow ribbon, and you cutting through the material with oversized ceremonial scissors, allowing the crowds at each end to approach each other and finally meet. And remember, if your traffic stalls in either direction or your bridge needs repair, talking with a therapist is a great way to keep your bridge open.

It's been good working with you.

Appendix
Progress Notes

_____
_____
_____
_____
_____
_____
_____
_____
_____
_____
_____
_____
_____
_____
_____
_____
_____
_____
_____
_____
_____
_____
_____
_____
_____
_____
_____
_____

Recommended Reading

Glover, R. A. *No More Mr. Nice Guy: A Proven Plan for Getting What You Want in Love, Sex, and Life.* Philadelphia: Running Press, 2003.

Hendrix, H. *Getting the Love You Want: A Guide for Couples.* New York: Harper and Row, 1988.

Henry, P. *The Emotionally Unavailable Man: A Blueprint for Healing.* Highland City, FL: Rainbow Books, 2004.

Pennebaker, J. W. *Opening Up: The Healing Power of Expressing Emotions.* New York: The Guilford Press, 1990.

Powell, D. *Playing Life's Second Half: A Man's Guide for Turning Success into Significance.* Oakland, CA: New Harbinger, 2003.

Real, T. *I Don't Want to Talk About It. Overcoming the Secret Legacy of Male Depression.* New York: Scribner, 1997.

Wall, C. L. *The Courage to Trust: A Guide to Building Deeper and Lasting Relationships.* Oakland, CA: New Harbinger, 2004.

Wexler, D. B. *When Good Men Behave Badly: Change Your Behavior, Change Your Relationships.* Oakland, CA: New Harbinger, 2004.

References

Bollas, C. 1987. *The Shadow of the Object: Psychoanalysis of the Unthought Known.* New York: Columbia University Press.

Bollas, C. 1995. *Cracking Up: The Work of Unconscious Experience.* London: Routledge.

Brantley, J. 2007. *Calming Your Anxious Mind: How Mindfulness and Compassion Can Free You from Anxiety, Fear and Panic.* Oakland, CA: New Harbinger.

Eifert, G. H., M. McKay, and J. Forsyth. 2006. *Act on Life Not on Anger: The New Acceptance and Commitment Therapy Guide to Problem Anger.* Oakland, CA: New Harbinger.

Greenson, R. R. 1967. *The Technique and Practice of Psychoanalysis.* 18th printing. Madison, CT: International University Press.

Hedges, L. E. 1994. *In Search of the Lost Mother of Infancy.* Northvale, NJ: Aaronson.

Hedges, L.E. (in press). *Cross-Cultural Encounters: Bridging Worlds of Difference.*

Jacobs, B. 2004. *Writing for Emotional Balance: A Guided Journal to Help You Manage Overwhelming Emotions.* Oakland, CA: New Harbinger.

Lejune, C. 2007. *The Worry Trap: How to Free Yourself from Worry and Anxiety Using Acceptance and Commitment Therapy.* Oakland, CA: New Harbinger.

McKay, M., and C. Sutker. 2005. *The Self-Esteem Guided Journal: A 10-Week Program*. Oakland, CA: New Harbinger.

Pennebaker, J. W. 2004. *Writing to Heal: A Guided Journal for Recovering from Trauma and Emotional Upheaval*. Oakland, CA: New Harbinger.

2093827

Made in the USA